MW01165673

"Yes and am
ately procla
sary call to
scripturally he has laid out our responsibility as the
church, to surrender our hearts again and become
truly usable to the Holy Spirit. The call is to be con-
victed and then to have that conviction move us
to our knees, once again pressing our great country through to a living faith...I say again, "Yes and
amen!"

—REVEREND JOHN SAENZ
ASSEMBLY OF GOD MISSIONARY TO SOUTHEAST ASIA

In *The Shaking of a Nation* Pastor Hill exposes the
dark side of America's heart, but he does it in the
light of God's mercy and plan for revival. Many
authors have rightfully exposed America's moral
collapse, but this is not just another finger-pointing
critique of our spiritual state. Pastor Hill offers hope
for our dilemma by revealing that God's judgment
is knocking on our national door but His mercy is
standing next to it. This book is a prophetic cry for
revival in America from the heart of a small-town
pastor who longs to see a national revival, one that
will "shake" this nation. A must-read!

—TOM BRAND
PASTOR, THE FATHER'S HOUSE
SAN SABA, TEXAS

Just as God chose an unknown man from a remote
village to bring His message of judgment and mercy
to that great city, Nineveh, so He has chosen an
unknown preacher from a remote town to bring
His message of judgment and mercy to this great
United States! God has not changed. His message
has not changed. Just as Nineveh listened, Christians across America must read and spread God's
message!

—JOHN GOODMAN
DEACON, MILFORD ASSEMBLY OF GOD
CINCINNATI, OHIO

We could truly sense the Spirit of God speaking through the pages of *The Shaking of a Nation*. God revealed to us that we are in need of more of His presence in all areas of our lives. We believe that those who read this book with an open heart for God's will in their lives shall also find that it will speak life into them. As God speaks into the lives and hearts of His people, the power of His change in us will bring the heart of the American church back to where it needs to be in order to fulfill His promises in our country.

—Jeff and Malia Turner
Members, Tri-County Assembly of God
Cincinnati, Ohio

Occasionally a book appears on the shelves of Christian bookstores that stirs the heart of every person who reads it. *The Shaking of a Nation* provides answers to questions that are of paramount importance to our great country. Could it be that there is a great move of God on the horizon and He is currently shaking everything that can be shaken? Is God now judging the United States for our great national sin? What can Americans expect to see in the near future? Reading *The Shaking of a Nation* will change your perspective on many things and cause you to greatly desire to return to the Lord with all your heart!

—David P. Hill Sr.
Pastor, Corinth Assembly of God
Corinth, Kentucky

# THE
# SHAKING
## OF A
# NATION

David P. Hill Jr.

CREATION
HOUSE
A STRANG COMPANY

Library of Congress Control Number: 2006923954
International Standard Book Number: 1-59979-009-2

First Edition

06 07 08 09 10 — 987654321
Printed in the United States of America

I dedicate *The Shaking of a Nation* to my Lord and Savior: You are the only One worthy of all the glory. I also dedicate this book to my dear wife Rebecca: you have always believed in me even when I doubted myself.

I wish to thank our families in Cincinnati for standing by Rebecca and me in the harvest of the Lord. I am eternally thankful for our friends Jeff and Malia who have supported us in so many ways. I also wish to thank San Saba First Assembly of God for being our family in Texas.

I finally dedicate this work to every reader: may *The Shaking of a Nation* bring great blessing to all who read its pages. May multitudes of Americans surrender to the grace of the Lord because of the words He has spoken through this book. America's hour of divine visitation is now at hand. All who will choose mercy instead of judgment will be blessed by the Lord.

# CONTENTS

# PREFACE

HAVE YOU EVER been in an earthquake? Although immediately prior to the earthquake everything seems to be secure and stable, this changes in a split second. Suddenly everything is being shaken and moved out of place. The stable structures that have been trusted for years suddenly begin to falter. People who were calm a moment ago are suddenly thrown into a panic because of the shaking all around them. During an earthquake, as in any natural disaster, our human nature causes us to immediately begin looking for a safe place.

I was quite an adventurous young man at age sixteen. I can still remember going with my dad to the Grand Canyon on vacation. While others at the canyon were content to simply peer over into the vast crevice from the ledges above, we were not. Instead we decided to take the twenty-four mile hike from the north rim to the south rim. Down into the canyon we hiked in the sweltering heat of that summer day. After going about ten miles we encountered something for which I was unprepared, but that I understand is quite common in the Grand Canyon.

The ground began suddenly to shake, rocks began to fall, and boulders began to move all around us deep in the inner canyon. I was caught completely off guard and suddenly this brave teenage explorer was looking for safety. My brush with those slight tremors was nothing compared to the awesome force of a real earthquake. Although I was not really in any grave danger the tremors I experienced that day left an impression on me about the destructive force of a real earthquake.

My friend, America has experienced some tremors in recent years. It seems that all we once thought was secure and stable has been shaken. We were all shaken through the school shootings of the nineties, the terrorist attacks (in our heartland first in 1995 and then in the terrible events of September 11, 2001), the corporate scandals in our most powerful companies, the war on terror overseas, and the terribly destructive storms that have come more frequently and with increasing force. All of these things have shaken us to the core and awakened us to the fact that the stability and freedom in which we have always trusted are actually quite fragile. The question I will answer throughout this book is: "Could there be a divine message for America in the tragic events of recent years?" The premise for this book is that a loving God does not delight in heartache and suffering, but there is a reason for His allowing calamity to come to America.

Even though we have courageously endured so much heartache, there is now a great anxiety about the future that has come upon many Americans. We seem to sense the worst is not yet over and an even greater tragedy is awaiting us just over the horizon. My fellow Americans, our country is being given a divine wake-up call. As a nation we have strayed far from the original intentions of our godly Founding Fathers. We were founded as a country where there could be freedom of religious expression in worship of Almighty God. We have twisted this freedom into an "anything goes" mentality. Instead of God being honored by the nation He established and blessed, He is ignored and even rejected. Some Americans are now actually taking legal action to get any mention of the one true God of heaven and earth out of every school, government building, and public place.

Suddenly the words *under God* and *in God we trust* have become offensive to some Americans. The court system that was designed to ensure "justice for all" is now being used as a tool to advance the opinions and agendas of Americans who have rejected the rule of God and the freedom that He has bestowed upon our great nation. Their desire is that all Americans embrace their opinions and ideas, which promise liberty, but reject the only God who can give true liberty. The current "terrorist attack" being leveled at our nation is an attack from within, upon the spiritual and moral fabric of America. The once-stable foundation of our great country trembles with each new, absurd legal case brought before our courts.

As our country continues its downward moral spiral, many God-fearing Americans are now asking a wonderful question: "Where is the God of our Founding Fathers?" Why does it seem the church of Jesus Christ is ineffective in this hour? Where is the powerful spiritual force that speaks to the heart of a society and turns it upside-down with the Gospel of Jesus Christ? Why does it seem the church is bent on making sure that Christians are comfortable and entertained, as our nation continues its tumble into a totally godless society? Most importantly, where is the power of God in this desperate hour and why is the church being used so greatly in other countries, but not in America? This book will expose biblical and Christ-centered answers to these questions.

To understand this book you must believe God still speaks to His people today, regarding the societies in which they live. This book will challenge every American's view of God. Through *The Shaking of a Nation*, the Lord will change the dedicated believer's view of Himself. Many American Christians no longer see God as His Word declares, in His true nature. This book will assume a biblical view of the one true God and Jesus Christ, His only Son.

Throughout these pages, God will reveal His tender heart for America but also His righteousness and justice. I anticipate two responses from those who read the message contained herein. The first is the deepest desire of God's heart: many will hear what God says to them through *The Shaking of a Nation*, and begin to pray in earnest for the United States of America. The call of the hour is for all who love God and country to fast, pray, and cry mightily unto God for the future and welfare of this great nation. The second response I anticipate from some who read this book is anger: I will be labeled judgmental, hateful, or even unpatriotic. I am fully prepared for such criticism. When God breaks the hearts of His people for their society they are often misunderstood, and how I am viewed is of no consequence to me.

As I write this book it occurs to me that some key national leaders may very well read it. I want to tell all of you who have the responsibility of leading our country that God will speak to you personally and clearly if you read this book with an open heart. You have been raised up by the Lord to your position of authority for this critical time in America and it is God's desire to use you to help bring healing to our land. I also am aware that many will read this book who do not yet know the Lord in a personal and real way. If you do not have a personal relationship with God through His only begotten Son Jesus, in the last chapter of this book you will be given instructions on how to begin one. If you do not truly know the Lord, understand His mercy toward you is great and He has arranged the circumstances of your life and this nation's calamity to bring you to Himself.

God has a wonderful plan for the United States of America and He wants us to respond to Him so we can see that plan come to pass. The message of *The Shaking of a Nation* is a message of hope. If we will turn to the Lord with all of our heart, with fasting and with prayer, He will turn to us again and bring lasting security and stability to our great country. If you are like me, you love America deeply. I don't know about you, but I am willing to fight for that which I love. This book will serve as a battle cry for all who love God and country to stand up and fight for what we treasure: our blessed union. I do not want to see America shaken any more than it has been. It is my desire to see peace in our land, quietness on our shores, and a bright future for our children. If we heed the call of 2 Chronicles 7:14, God will bring America back to her former glory and we can once again be a blessed country that is truly "one nation under God."

> If my people who are called by my name humble themselves, and pray and seek my face, and turn from their wicked ways, then I will hear from heaven, and will forgive their sin and heal their land.
>
> —2 CHRONICLES 7:14, RSV

one

# LISTEN TO THE SHAKING

And His voice shook the earth then, but now
He has promised, saying, "Yet once more I
will shake not only the earth, but also the
heaven."

—HEBREWS 12:26, NAS

## God Is Speaking Through the Shaking

We have felt the shaking in America today, but have we
listened? It seems the precious freedom and security,
which we once thought were firmly established, are now
in jeopardy. We were shocked when teenagers went on
mass shootings at their school. Hundreds were sense-
lessly murdered by terrorism in Oklahoma City. Then the
events of September 11, 2001, shook every American to
the core as we marveled at the evil in the hearts of those
who hate our freedom.

It seems there is now less trust in the business world
because of the shockwaves caused by greedy men. Many
American parents have been shaken with grief as military personnel have come to their homes with news of
a brave, fallen soldier. Powerful storms have wreaked
havoc as they have shaken our shores. Many Americans
were heartbroken as Hurricane Katrina devastated one of
our beloved cities and caused catastrophic loss of life and
property. Prior to Katrina, who would have believed we

1

would have to use sports stadiums for refugee camps in the United States?

It seems many events of recent years have made us stronger and more unified as a nation. However, there is a burning question in all of our hearts now: "Could there be a divine message in all of this?" Why does it seem our freedom has become so fragile and our security so jeopardized? Where is God in all of the shaking and what does He want us to know through the tears and tragedy? Although no one understands why we must suffer sometimes, God always offers us comfort. This is the message of the Bible, that God is a very near source of peace and safety. When everything around us is being shaken, He is the Rock that cannot be shaken. My friend, if America will turn to God we will find safety in His loving care. It is not a time to draw back in fear, but time to rise up in faith and be all that God has called us to be as a country. God is speaking through the shaking. Are we listening?

This book is being written to answer some of the questions many of us have right now. God does have a message for us through all of the shaking we have felt in this nation during the last decade. He is calling us to hear His voice once again. It is never God's desire for us to live with heartache and pain. He does, however, allow suffering to overwhelm us in order to cause us to turn to Him. He wants us to listen to Him speak His peace into our lives, even through the instability of the shaking we feel all around us.

## One Nation, Under God?

America is an awesome country. The freedoms we enjoy in the workplace, in worship, and in recreation have been a continual blessing from the Lord. Few nations have had as rich a spiritual heritage as ours. Few nations have had as much divine providence as the United States of America. God has provided for us in our times of greatest need. He has protected us in our times of greatest crises. He has fought with us in our times of greatest conflict. When we needed God the most, He stood by our side as we have declared we are "one nation under God." He has also sent us many of His servants to share His heart and His message throughout our history.

We have been so very blessed spiritually. Few nations were born in the fires of spiritual revolution and revival as we were. Few nations have been as completely saturated with the Gospel as we have. Few nations have had so many Christian churches as we have. Few nations have had so many powerful preachers as we have. Few nations have had revival after revival after revival, as we have. With all of the spiritual light that God has given us you would think we would have the most Christ-centered nation on earth. This is not the case, however, and the nation that was created by God for His purpose is now being shaken because of our own rebellion against heaven.

As a nation we have fallen from the divine grace upon which we were founded. We have been given such a wonderful freedom and we have abused it. Instead of using our liberty to serve the only true God, we have used it to form gods according to our own desires. America is no longer "one nation under God," but "one nation under gods." Instead of serving the Lord, we are serving the gods of self, greed, lust, power, and violence. Do we think that we will not be held accountable for these things? Today we use our freedom to practice open rebellion against the very God who gave us our great nation. Our land has been saturated with the light of God, and yet we choose to walk in darkness. The Bible makes it very clear that when we are given much, we will be required to give an account of the same. America is responsible for a lot more than most nations because of the blessings God has graciously provided. We were not founded as a spiritually dark nation that embraced false religion. We were founded as a nation that honored God and embraced the Gospel of Christ. If we listen to the shaking, it will tell us that our day of reckoning is now at hand. Our loving Creator is calling out to us, *Turn, every one of you, from self, greed, lust, power, and violence. Return to Me and I will have mercy on you. For I am gracious and forgiving, and I will abundantly pardon.*

We were founded as a nation where people could worship the true God in any way they chose. We have perverted that spiritual freedom into a rebellious lifestyle. Most Americans feel their freedom entitles them to live their lives by any whim they choose. Many now believe our liberty teaches us that in the United States every belief is given equal approval. Please do not misunderstand me here, we should never discriminate or persecute anyone for their beliefs, but neither should we say that every belief is right and correct. Look at the laws of the universe. They teach us there are opposites such as light and darkness and life and death. Do we not understand that just as there are physical opposites in the universe, so there are spiritual opposites? There is a spiritual light and a spiritual darkness, there is a God and a Satan, there is a heaven and a hell. All who chose to reject the light of Jesus Christ as the only living God embrace the kingdom of darkness—and the United States is currently making that terrible choice.

In spite of all the shaking, we still feel that our freedom teaches us we should never speak out against a fellow American's lifestyle or beliefs. This mentality has allowed a law to stand for over thirty years that grants people the right to decide whether their children should be born and also grants doctors a right to take the lives of unwanted babies. We have drifted so very far from our godly heritage and the Christ-likeness of our Founding Fathers.

## The Terrible Price of Our Rebellion

Sin is not a popular word in America today. Although its effects can be seen everywhere, somehow people feel more secure denying its existence. Maybe what we really have a hard time with is admitting we have all sinned. The best biblical definition for sin is "missing the mark." We have all missed God's mark or purpose for our lives at some point. Sin is also rebellion against a loving Creator. We have all, to some degree, lived our lives in rebellion against God. Romans 3:23 assures us that "all have sinned, and come short of the glory of God." This is perhaps the most terrible effect of sin: we miss God's glory. When we remain in sin, we do not enjoy the peace and presence of God that He longs for each of us to know. The terrible price of sin and doing things "our way" is that it separates us from the loving God who created us.

The Bible declares that the payment for sin is death. (See Romans 6:23.) Sin separates us from God now and for eternity. Just as sin will separate an individual from the presence of God, so will it separate a nation from His blessing. The effects of sin are all around us in a country that is bent on doing its own will instead of God's will. Just as there are personal sins against God that carry grave consequences, so there are national sins against Him that carry consequences. If we listen to the shaking in America it will tell us that we are beginning to pay the price for our national sins. The shaking and uneasiness we have all felt recently are because God's hand of blessing and protection is being removed from a country that

**5**

is living in open rebellion and sin.

The good news through all of this is the Holy Spirit is here to reveal our sin. When God shows us our sin it is always for our benefit and well-being. The proper response to the convicting work of the Spirit is to repent. Repentance involves a turning away from sin and self and a turning to God in faith. Just as the Holy Spirit calls individuals to repent from sin and turn to God through Christ, so He also calls nations. I believe such a call is going out across America today. From sea to shining sea, the shaking in our land is telling us, "Repent, for God's judgment is near."

## It Is Time to Listen to the Shaking

The increasingly frequent tremors America is feeling today are actually the Lord calling us to repentance because He is a God of justice and mercy. Many seem willing to see only His mercy, but the same Bible that describes God as a loving Creator also describes Him as a just Judge. My friend, these two things always have existed side-by-side in this world: God's judgment and God's mercy. Be assured that He delights in mercy and His judgment is an act of that mercy. His judgment is intended to call sinners to the attention of His holiness and bring them into right standing before God. This right standing is found only through a personal and passionate faith-relationship with His only begotten Son, Jesus Christ.

God is shaking our nation and trying to wake us up so we will recognize His calling us into a relationship with Christ. I already hear the argument from some well-meaning people that, "God is loving, and doesn't send disaster, war, or hurricanes as part of His judgment." What does the Bible say concerning this though? Listen to Isaiah 45:7, "I form the light and create darkness, I make peace and create calamity; I, the LORD, do all these things" (NKJV). The word *calamity* means misfortune or even great distress. My friend, those two words describe many of the events that have taken place in our nation recently. We must believe the Lord and see His hand in all of these things that have come upon us.

America today stands at the threshold of a great and terrible judgment. We have walked in disobedience too long. We have rejected God and sought to get Him out of every area of our public and private lives. It has been said that God is a just Judge and His justice will not sleep forever. His justice is the reason that Jesus had to die on the cross for our sins. The holy life of the Righteous One had to be given to pay our sin debt owed to God. Jesus is called the "friend of sinners" in Matthew 11:19. He is full of compassion for those who have gone astray. However, we must realize that the same Bible that calls Jesus the "friend of sinners" also says that, "God is angry with the wicked every day" (Ps. 7:11). Although He has forgiven millions through the ages, He cannot forgive the one who does not come to Him through Christ. It is time for America to come to God through Christ and to repent for the sin that has shaken our land. The justice that awaits us can be avoided if we repent and accept Christ's sacrifice as payment for our national sin.

Is the shaking we have felt recently really the full judgment of God in order to destroy the United States of America? Absolutely not. If God had already judged America she would be in complete ruins today and unable to rise again. Do we really understand the power of God? If God wanted to destroy America He could do so with ease. No, God is not bent on our destruction but on our restoration. Having said all of that, let me share with you that what is coming on our nation is much worse than any recent event that we have suffered. If America does not turn from its sin God's judgment will surely fall.

We have felt the shaking in America today, but have we listened to it? We keep feeling the tremors as the unstable ground shifts beneath us and we keep hardening our hearts. God is speaking to us through the calamity we have gone through as a nation. It is time to turn to the Lord to hear what He is saying to the United States of America. It is time to listen to the shaking.

## two

# A DIVINE WARNING

If that nation against whom I have spoken turns from its evil, I will relent of the disaster that I thought to bring upon it. And the instant I speak concerning a nation and concerning a kingdom, to build and to plant it, if it does evil in My sight so that it does not obey My voice, then I will relent concerning the good with which I said I would benefit it.

—JEREMIAH 18:8–11, NKJV

## Our Greatest National Sin

The shaking we have all felt in America over the last several years has been a divine warning. An awesome and terrible judgment is coming soon to the United States of America. It is God's desire that America turn to the Lord with all of her heart now and avoid this disaster. God is mercifully giving us an opportunity to repent of our sin and to make a choice to become "one nation under God" again. Do we realize what that phrase means? We are called to be one nation, submitted to the plan and power of a loving Creator. What a wonderful Christian heritage we have, as expressed in those words from our Pledge of Allegiance.

America has fallen headlong into a great national sin. The Bible lists seven sins that can only be described as a "slap in the face" to a loving God. It is the purpose of this chapter to expose one of these sins that we are practicing in America today. I will mention two others first here, just to show how they digress into the third. Listen to this verse from the writings of the wisest person who ever lived, King Solomon:

> There are six things which the LORD hates, seven which are an abomination to him: haughty eyes, a lying tongue, and hands that shed innocent blood.
> —PROVERBS 6:16–17, RSV

According to this Scripture there are certain sins that offend heaven more than others. It is one thing to sin in ignorance, it is another to willfully practice sin. Willful sinning is always prideful rebellion against the Lord, described here in this verse as "haughty eyes." This type of sin is committed when we harden our hearts against the revealed will and sovereignty of a merciful God. If we allow this pride in our hearts our lives quickly become perverted and we fail to recognize the truth of God. In Proverbs 6:17, this state is described as "a lying tongue." Trapped in this condition we begin to lie to ourselves about what is right and what is wrong.

Many in our nation no longer recognize that there are moral absolutes. A lot of Americans no longer believe there are things that are wrong simply because God says they are. When a society begins to walk in prideful rebellion against God and no longer recognizes the truth of God, only terrible things can follow. Suddenly the truth of the precious nature of human life disappears. When a nation begins to devalue peoples' lives, the innocent always suffer. The weak are taken advantage of by the strong. King Solomon expressed this abomination as "hands that shed innocent blood."

Since 1973 more than forty-seven million unborn babies have been legally murdered in America. Let me make something clear at this point: the purpose of this chapter is not to condemn any individual who has had an abortion, nor is it to condemn a particular political party. The purpose here is to expose our greatest national sin. It is not a Democratic sin or a Republican sin, but a national sin. The United States is guilty in the eyes of the Lord because we have allowed *Roe v. Wade* to stand for all of these years. The cries of nearly fifty million innocent children have ascended before the throne of a loving and merciful God. He would have to be a ruthless God to not respond in His justice to the cries of the unborn. I am not going to make an argument at this point for the sanctity of human life. I will simply make the statement that all life is precious before God.

## Their Blood Is on Our Hands

Heaven is looking down today and it sees the blood of forty-seven million innocent babies on the hands of the United States. Yes, there are many people who love God and serve Him in America. As a nation, however, we are all guilty of this abomination in the eyes of the Lord. There are good Christians who are committed to the cause of Christ in this country, but as a whole the church has looked the other way as millions of babies have been "legally" killed. If we were a spiritually darkened country practicing witchcraft or a nation in which a false religion was predominant, perhaps our guilt would be less in the Lord's eyes. The simple fact of the matter is that we know better in America. We were founded as a Christian nation with Christian morals. We were founded by divine decree as a nation that would embrace and promote the Gospel of Christ. Again, as Jesus declared nearly two thousand years ago, "to whom much is given, of him will much be required" (Luke 12:48, RSV). God now is giving us a clear warning that it is time to repent of the violence that is in our hands and to embrace the Gospel of Jesus as a nation again.

You may be reading this and saying, "I have never had an abortion, I do not even believe that it is right. Surely I am not guilty for this sin." While every American may not be guilty of this sin before the Lord, we are all responsible. The question is not, "Do you believe abortion is right?" The question is, "Are you an American?" As Americans we each have an individual responsibility to end the shedding of innocent blood in our country. It is time for all those who love America and who believe the Word of the Lord to rise up and fight for the innocents. In the next chapter I will plead with the church and all true believers in Jesus to take action concerning our horrific national sin.

The Bible tells us in the Book of Isaiah that God calls all the stars in the sky by name. (See Isaiah 40:26.) How much more does He remember the names of the babies that are murdered every day in America? These lives may be worthless to our nation, but God places a high value on them. He knows each one's exact life span. He knows the gifts and talents He deposited into each soul. He knows the person He wanted these children to marry, the place where He wanted them to live, and the friendships He wanted them to have. The Bible tells us that God has intimate knowledge of us from our conception. (See Psalm 139:13–16.) Even before these babies' lives began He knew and loved them. He knows every hair on their heads, the color of their eyes, and every thought they would ever have during their earthly life. Each baby murdered in America is precious in the eyes of our Creator. It is because of His great love for all His children, born and unborn, that God right now is so aggrieved by our nation.

## Our Courts and the Court of Heaven

American law has exalted itself above the law of Almighty God. When we passed *Roe v. Wade* we were telling the Lord that a baby's life is not important and unborn children are not valuable. We told God that a person's right to choose whether or not they wanted to have a baby is more important than that child's right to live. The court in the United States today looks at "the constitutional right to an abortion" as a settled issue. The court of heaven, led by the righteous Judge Himself, has never acknowledged or validated that decision. God is calling every American and every leader in our government to reconsider *Roe v. Wade* carefully in the light of His Word. He is also calling our judges to begin fighting for the cause of the innocent. There are many good and godly judges in America. Unfortunately their decisions are often overlooked because of the wickedness of others in authority.

The following illustration[1] clearly shows the extent of our national sin. The current population of the shaded states is equal to the number of babies that have been "legally" killed in our nation since the landmark 1973 *Roe v. Wade* decision:

The words of the prophet Jeremiah apply to America's court system today as much as they did to Old Testament Israel:

> They are waxen fat, they shine: yea, they overpass the deeds of the wicked: they judge not the cause, the cause of the fatherless, yet they prosper; and the right of the needy do they not judge. Shall I not visit for these things? saith the LORD: shall not my soul be avenged on such a nation as this?
> —JEREMIAH 5:28–29

Today in America our courts pardon the wicked. Celebrities go free even after they have committed child molestation and murder. Meanwhile, the rights of the needy are overlooked. The innocent children who have no money or prestige in our nation also have no voice in our judicial system. None of these things have gone unnoticed in heaven. Until we repent for our national sin and become a Christ-centered nation again His judgments will continue to fall with increasing frequency and force. The Lord will now repay the innocent blood that we have shed throughout our land. As God said to Jeremiah concerning Israel, so He is saying to the church concerning the United States:

> Shall I not visit for these things... shall not my soul be avenged on such a nation as this?
> —JEREMIAH 5:29

## Judgment Is Almost Here

I have no idea what form the coming judgment on the United States will take. God has revealed to me that it is coming very soon, though. On June 26, 2005, I was awakened by the Spirit of the Lord in the middle of the night and given this divine revelation: *The sins of the United States and the shedding of innocent blood have come up before Me. I am now going to give America one year in which to repent and then I am going to utter my judgments against her.*

The force and conviction of this message echoed in my heart for weeks after this divine visitation. Immediately I received an awesome burden for America and I began to pray in earnest for our welfare. I also began to pray and search the Scriptures for answers. God began to remind me through His Word that He still rules the nations. He still judges entire countries in order to get people to turn to Him through Christ. Whenever God speaks concerning such a matter it is always important to look for confirmation. As I sought Him for such a sign the Holy Spirit showed me a powerful confirmation within a matter of just a few days.

Justice Sandra Day O'Connor resigned suddenly from the Supreme Court on Friday, July 1, 2005. She is a moderate conservative, but more importantly she had been a pro-choice swing vote on abortion issues. Her resignation and the shaking that has taken place in the Supreme Court is nothing less than a window of grace for our nation to repent for the shedding of innocent blood. Our fasting, prayers, and repentance are the keys if *Roe v. Wade* is to be overturned. America has been graciously given a divine window of grace from July 2005 to July 2006 in which to repent for "the shedding of innocent blood."

## History Is Our Example

Take a hard look at history and see how God dealt with other nations that hardened their hearts against Him. Does He still do so today? Is He still the Judge of the nations? Unless you are a deist (who believes God is far away and uninvolved in human affairs), the answer is

15

yes. Look at rebellious Israel that was judged and over-thrown again and again. Look at the other hardhearted nations against whom God uttered His judgments in the Bible. Look at the judgment pronounced on the unrepentant cities by Jesus during His earthly ministry. Look at the former Soviet Union just a few years ago. The U.S.S.R. rejected God from its government for seventy years and today its people are paying the price. I am told by Christians who have visited the former Soviet Union that two extremes exist side-by-side: revival and despair. Much of the church in that part of the world is having a revival even as more and more disillusioned countrymen slip into the despair of alcohol and drug abuse. May God save America from such a day and may we repent now for the "shedding of innocent blood."

If we really understood the power God has over the nations every American would cry out to the Lord in desperation and pray, "Spare our country, O God." He alone is responsible for raising up one nation and judging another. He exalts one leader or government and overthrows another. Even when one country wages war against another and removes its leader or government the hand of the Lord is always present. This may come as a shock to many reading this book, but the government of the United States was not ultimately responsible for making the decision to remove Saddam Hussein from power. Listen to what the Bible clearly teaches on this subject:

> For promotion cometh neither from the east, nor from the west, nor from the south. But God is the judge: he putteth down one, and setteth up another.
> —PSALM 75:6–7

## A Prophetic Message

Many readers by now may have felt a reaction to the prophetic message contained in this book. There is the reaction of anger and doubt, but also of conviction, weeping, and repentance. God is calling each of us to forsake our anger and doubt and to embrace with contrite hearts the Word that He is now speaking to America. His desire is for healing and He warns us of the consequence of our sin so that we will turn to Him. My fellow Americans, God wants only mercy and not judgment come to our nation. Does God really speak to His people today concerning the society in which they live? Of course He does—He "is the same yesterday, today, and forever" (Heb. 13:8, NKJV). What does the Word of God teach us regarding this subject?

> Surely the Lord GOD does nothing, unless He reveals His secret to His servants the prophets. A lion has roared! Who will not fear? The Lord GOD has spoken. Who can but prophesy?
>
> —AMOS 3:7–8, NKJV

According to this verse, God will not do anything until He gives His people notice first. Why are we given notice? So we can then fast, pray, and warn. So God can change the hearts of men, women, and even entire nations through our prayers and faith. Most of us have heard the story of the prophet Jonah. However, I wonder if we have missed the purpose of what God is speaking to us through that Old Testament story. The message of Jonah shows us plainly that God gives people a "space" in which to repent. In Nineveh's case God told them that it was only forty days. What was their response? Let's look at a passage from the Book of Jonah:

So the people of Nineveh believed God, and proclaimed a fast, and put on sackcloth, from the
greatest of them even to the least of them. For word
came unto the king of Nineveh, and he arose from
his throne, and he laid his robe from him, and covered him with sackcloth, and sat in ashes. And he
caused it to be proclaimed and published through
Nineveh by the decree of the king and his nobles,
saying, Let neither man nor beast, herd nor flock,
taste any thing: let them not feed, nor drink water:
But let man and beast be covered with sackcloth,
and cry mightily unto God: yea, let them turn every
one from his evil way, and from the violence that
is in their hands. Who can tell if God will turn and
repent, and turn away from his fierce anger, that
we perish not? And God saw their works, that they
turned from their evil way; and God repented of the
evil, that he had said that he would do unto them;
and he did it not.

—JONAH 3:5–10

## How Will We Respond?

Jesus is walking throughout our land right now and
pleading with us to turn from our greatest national sin. It
is time to respond to His voice through the shaking. May
we not harden our hearts and suffer the same fate as the
other nations and people groups to whom He spoke in
times past. May we not hear the words of Matthew 12
that Jesus spoke to those who heard His words, yet were
unrepentant:

The men of Nineveh will rise up in the judgment
with this generation and condemn it, because they
repented at the preaching of Jonah; and indeed a
greater than Jonah is here. The queen of the South
will rise up in the judgment with this generation

and condemn it, for she came from the ends of the earth to hear the wisdom of Solomon; and indeed a greater than Solomon is here.

—Matthew 12: 41–42, nkjv

So what can we do about any of these things? We who truly believe in the Lord can begin to repent for the United States. Let me make this very clear: God is giving the believers in America an opportunity to intercede. At the same time God is giving our government an opportunity to repent of the decision called *Roe v. Wade*. The biblical concept of repentance means a total and complete change of heart and mind toward God. There is no compromise on this point: *Roe v. Wade* must be overturned if our nation is to be spared. God is not requiring new legislation that will limit certain types of abortions or new parental consent laws for young women who desire an abortion. He is requiring our government to say, "We were wrong and we now repent before God." As the Lord gives people a "space" and an opportunity in which to repent, so He has done for our nation. The prophetic word of this book is not a mystery, it is a clear word: an awesome judgment will fall upon America in the summer of 2006. Then God will continue to shake our land until we repent and turn to Him. May our faith rise up and be strong enough to overcome the evil that is destroying our land. May the innocents be given the right to live. May the United States repent and not be judged by the Lord.

> For the nation and kingdom that will not serve thee shall perish; yea, those nations shall be utterly wasted.
>
> —Isaiah 60:12

**three**

# STANDING IN THE GAP

"So I sought for a man among them who would make a wall, and stand in the gap before Me on behalf of the land, that I should not destroy it; but I found no one. Therefore I have poured out My indignation on them; I have consumed them with the fire of My wrath; and I have recompensed their deeds on their own heads," says the Lord GOD.
—EZEKIEL 22:30–31, NKJV

## The Lost Ministry of Intercession

In the midst of all the rebellion, shaking, and violence in America today there is still hope. This hope is not found in a political party, social reform, military might, a police force, or even in a religion. America's hope is only found in remembering our former years. We must go back to the place where this nation was founded: faith in Jesus Christ. We need to return with all of our heart to the faith of our Founding Fathers. This will never be possible without somebody standing in the gap for this great country. According to Ezekiel 22:30–31 there is a massive "gap" between God and the societies upon which He pronounces His judgment. The good news, according to this same Scripture, is that God is actively looking for someone to "stand" in that gap.

The Lord is looking for Christians in America who will share His burden and intercede for our backsliding nation. Webster's Dictionary defines the term *intercession* as "an entreaty or prayer on the behalf of others." God is seeking Christians who will intercede by fasting and praying (see chapter 6) on behalf of the United States of America. He is looking for someone who will be a bridge between Himself and a nation that has gone astray. If the church in America will seek God on behalf of our country, then He will use us to usher in another great awakening. If we answer the call for intercession, He will use us to speak to the soul of a nation that is shaking beneath the weight of His judgment. This is always the biblical pattern of intercession: we plead with God on behalf of man and then we plead with man on behalf of God.

Many pastors and teachers are missing the mark in the area of intercession today. God has called those of us who serve His church to be examples to our congregations in the ministry of intercession. It is far too easy to delegate this ministry to someone else instead of being the example that God desires for us to be to the church. May the leaders of the church in America rise up with a new determination to intercede for our congregations, our cities, and our nation. May we follow the examples of Abraham, Moses, Samuel, and our Great Shepherd Jesus who all prayed fervently for those whom God had entrusted to their pastoral care. How can we expect our churches to intercede and stand in the gap when we ourselves are not setting the pace?

The Lord is searching for those in the church who will take up the lost ministry of intercession. Today the average church in America eats together more than it prays together. We are more concerned with saving "doctrinal purity" than we are about the salvation of a nation. We are more concerned with debating worship styles than we are about a country that has forgotten God. We are more concerned with "who is in control" in our churches than we are about God's broken heart for the United States. My friends, these things ought not be so and it is time for the true believers in Jesus to stand in the gap for a country that is being shaken by the wrath of God.

Where are the intercessors who are walking in God's authority today? Where is the prophetic church that speaks to an apostate government with God's authority like Elijah of old? Where is the church whose prayer is so effective that people are spared God's judgment as when Moses prayed? (See Numbers 14:19–20.) America's church knows a lot about the power of man and very little about the power of God. We have hundreds of seminars on how to "do church" better, but where is our passion to know God's heart? In the midst of all of our new programs, cutting-edge technology, and ministry flowcharts, where are the tears of intercession? Where is the fasting, prayer, and weeping that will transform a nation with the love of Christ? God is calling us to return to our lost ministry of intercession.

The first Christians were passionate about prayer and intercession. Such a pattern can quickly be seen by a brief look at the Book of Acts. The early church was so dedicated to the ministry of prayer that God used them to shake the society in which they lived. These radical Christians literally turned the world upside down with their heartfelt cries to heaven. Where are the churches in America that are taking up the lost ministry of intercession?

## The Pattern Given by Jesus

Jesus Christ is not only our Lord and Savior, but also our example in all things. In the ministry of intercession He has blazed a trail in the Spirit for us and shown us the way. There was a time when none of us could possibly come before God. All of humanity was lost and on the way to eternal separation from God because of both our original and willful sin. Through the sin of Adam and our own choice the human race had an enormous gap between itself and the Father of Creation. Jesus came into the world and died for our sin and thus bridged that gap that had separated us from our Maker. He became the ultimate Intercessor and gave His precious blood at Calvary in order to "stand in the gap" between sinful man and a holy God. Jesus is still our great Intercessor today. Listen to the Book of Hebrews as it describes His ministry for us all:

> Wherefore he is able also to save them to the uttermost that come unto God by him, seeing he ever liveth to make intercession for them.
> —HEBREWS 7:25

I already hear the argument of some Christians, "Well that's Jesus, but intercession is just not my ministry." Let me tell you something, believer: if you are saved, you are called to be an intercessor. If Jesus is your Lord and Master you are called to bring people back to God. None of us could have died for the sins of humanity and bridged the gap between God and mankind as Jesus did two thousand years ago; however, we can answer the call of the Holy Spirit today to stand in the gap for the United States. For what purpose has God saved us and left us here on earth (for the time being) if not to intercede for the societies in which we live? If the church in America does not fast, pray, and stand in the gap for our country then nobody will.

God has always called intercessors to stand between Himself and sinners to share His great love for them.

There is not a man or woman of God in the Bible that was not called to transform the society or nation in which he or she lived. As New Testament Christians we have God's full revelation of His will for humanity. The church has been given more revelation of who God is through Christ than even the Lord's Old Testament prophets were given. In our Lord and Savior we have a more complete revelation of God's nature than even the angels in heaven. (See 1 Peter 1:12.)

What have we done with this great and awesome privilege in the American church? Is the church passionately in love with Jesus and totally committed to His ministry of intercession? Just read the weekly bulletin from almost any church in the United States and you will see that prayer is not even a priority, let alone the order of the day. Fellowship meals, choir practices, youth meetings, children's church, and outreaches all have their place in the agenda of the local church. Intercessory prayer, however, is missing, much to the dismay of heaven. May the church in America return to the pattern that has been set before us by Jesus, our great Intercessor.

## A Pattern of Intercession From the Beginning

Without intercessors calling out to the Lord on behalf of the United States, our nation has no hope of being spared God's judgment. The Lord has already declared His intent to hold us accountable for our rebellion against Him and the shedding of innocent blood. He is now calling the church in America to intercede and stand in the gap on behalf of the land. Whenever the sin of any people reaches its fullness it comes up in heaven before the throne of God. He then always calls His people to the ministry of intercession with Him. God's desire is always mercy and never judgment. We can see this truth clearly in the first book of the Bible. Listen to a peculiar event from the life of Abraham as it is recorded in the Book of Genesis:

> The Lord said, "Shall I hide from Abraham what I am about to do, seeing that Abraham shall become a great and mighty nation, and all the nations of the earth shall bless themselves by him? No, for I have chosen him, that he may charge his children and his household after him to keep the way of the Lord by doing righteousness and justice; so that the Lord may bring to Abraham what he has promised him."
> —Genesis 18:17–19, rsv

God begins this passage by asking a question. I want you to know that God never asks a question because He is in need of an answer. The only time God asks a question is when He is trying to teach His children something. When God asked Adam in the Garden of Eden, "Where are you?" He wasn't looking for him as we would look for lost car keys. He was trying to teach Adam that his sin had separated himself and Eve from their loving Creator. The desire of our Lord is to teach His servants His way and to let them share His burden. Listen once again to the question that God asks in this passage from the Book of Genesis, "Shall I hide from Abraham what I am about to do, seeing that Abraham shall become a great and mighty nation, and all the nations of the earth shall bless themselves by him?" (Gen. 18:17–18, rsv).

The Lord is getting ready to speak to Abraham concerning His judgment on Sodom and Gomorrah and His question is rhetorical. He answers Himself so He can teach Abraham His purpose, "No, for I have chosen him, that he may charge his children and his household after him to keep the way of the Lord by doing righteousness and justice; so that the Lord may bring to Abraham what he has promised him" (Gen. 18:19, RSV). The Lord answers His own question by stating He has chosen Abraham to "keep the way of the LORD" and also teach it to all who will follow in his footsteps of faith. What is the "way of the Lord" that God is speaking of in this passage? It is the way that He involves His children in what He is doing in the earth by our sharing in His "righteousness and justice." At no point in the history of the world has God ever hidden His plans and His intentions from His people. Abraham was given intimate knowledge of God's future actions because he walked closely with Him. The church in America has been called into the same close relationship with God through His Son. He wants us to share in what He is doing today.

## A Divine Audience

"Then the LORD said, 'Because the outcry against Sodom and Gomorrah is great and their sin is very grave, I will go down to see whether they have done altogether according to the outcry which has come to me; and if not, I will know.' So the men turned from there, and went toward Sodom; but Abraham still stood before the LORD" (Gen. 18:20–22, RSV).

What a powerful passage from Genesis. Here we see the Lord getting ready to destroy a society because of their sin and He doesn't even act until He speaks with Abraham about it. I wonder if there are any Christians in America today who are walking that closely to the Lord? Let me tell you that we have a better covenant with God than Abraham could have ever dreamed of having.

In his relationship with God Abraham had to look forward to the new covenant, but we have been freely given that covenant and access into the very throne room of God through the blood of Christ. On earth, Abraham never saw the fulfillment of his faith in God (see Hebrews 11:39–40), but today we see Jesus as the complete and total Revelation of God's nature. Jesus is the sure Foundation upon whom our covenant relationship with God is now based. If God did not hide what He was about to do from Abraham, how much less will He hide His intentions from believers in America today? Our problem is that we are not listening, but rest assured God is still speaking.

In this passage, God begins to reveal His intentions to Abraham concerning the judgment of a wicked society. Why does the Lord use prophecy to show us what He intends to do? So we can respond to Him by interceding. Here, God tells Abraham there is an outcry against Sodom and Gomorrah and their sin is very grave. He then says something strange: "I will go down to see whether they have done altogether according to the outcry which has come to me; and if not, I will know" (Gen. 18:21, RSV).

## An Opportunity to Intercede

Why in the world would an all-knowing God need to "go down to see" if the cry against Sodom and Gomorrah was accurate? We need to understand that He was coming down for Abraham and Sodom's benefit, not for His own. He was about to give Abraham the opportunity to be an intercessor and to stand in the gap. He was about to give Abraham an audience and allow him to intercede for a society that had crossed a divine line in the sand. Oh, how we need intercessors in America to respond like Abraham did to the call of God! Listen to his faith as described by his immediate response to the Lord:

> Then Abraham drew near, and said, "Wilt thou indeed destroy the righteous with the wicked? Suppose there are fifty righteous within the city; wilt thou then destroy the place and not spare it for the

fifty righteous who are in it? Far be it from thee
to do such a thing, to slay the righteous with the
wicked, so that the righteous fare as the wicked!
Far be that from thee! Shall not the Judge of all the
earth do right?"

—Genesis 18:23–25, RSV

At this point in the story we see the beautiful ministry of intercession beginning. Abraham "drew near"
and began to call "the righteous" to God's attention. He
asks God if He will still destroy the city if there are only
fifty in it who are truly serving Him. Abraham felt that
surely God would not destroy righteous people with the
wicked. Notice that Abraham appeals to God's justice
in this matter, "Shall not the Judge of all the earth do
right?" No, God's justice would not allow His servants to
be destroyed with those who had hardened their hearts
against Him. There is, however, a more important matter on the Lord's heart in this passage, the salvation of
a wicked society. Listen to God's mercy as expressed in
Abraham's intercession:

And the Lord said, "If I find at Sodom fifty righteous in the city, I will spare the whole place for
their sake." Abraham answered, "Behold, I have
taken upon myself to speak to the Lord, I who am
but dust and ashes. Suppose five of the fifty righteous are lacking? Wilt thou destroy the whole city
for lack of five?" And he said, "I will not destroy it if
I find forty-five there." Again he spoke to him, and
said, "Suppose forty are found there." He answered,
"For the sake of forty I will not do it." Then he said,
"Oh let not the Lord be angry, and I will speak. Suppose thirty are found there." He answered, "I will
not do it, if I find thirty there." He said, "Behold, I
have taken upon myself to speak to the Lord. Sup-

pose twenty are found there." He answered, "For the sake of twenty I will not destroy it." Then he said, "Oh let not the Lord be angry, and I will speak again but this once. Suppose ten are found there." He answered, "For the sake of ten I will not destroy it." And the LORD went his way, when he had finished speaking to Abraham; and Abraham returned to his place.

—GENESIS 18:26–33, RSV

My friend, can you hear the compassion of the Lord in this passage? Can you hear the mercy of a wonderful heavenly Father as Abraham intercedes? God is looking for a reason to spare Sodom. He says, "Yes, if I find fifty, forty-five, forty, thirty, twenty, yes, even only ten righteous people there, I will not destroy it for their sake" (Gen. 18:26–33, author's paraphrase). Why would God leave these righteous there and spare a society that had rebelled against His Word? It is because He was bent on the salvation of Sodom and Gomorrah and not on their destruction.

Yes, God would leave ten righteous people there with the desire that they reach their wicked neighbors. Why does the Lord say if there are enough righteous people in the society, it will be spared? He says this because if there is any chance a society can be reached by His people, He will spare that society and give the righteous a divine opportunity to intercede and share His message.

## An Opportunity to Repent

Just as Abraham was given a divine audience, so the church in America is being given an opportunity to intercede for our country. At the same time, America is also being given an opportunity to repent. How many righteous people will it take for the Lord to spare the United States? That is up to Him, but the more believers that cry out to God on behalf of a nation in rebellion, the better that nation's opportunity to repent. How long before God stops giving us wake-up calls and decides to completely overthrow the United States? Only God knows, but the church in America is being called to intercede regardless of God's foreknowledge concerning His judgment.

May we follow the pattern set before us in the Old Testament in the life of Abraham. More importantly, may we respond to the call of God to intercede and follow the great Intercessor, our blessed Savior. As God is calling the church to stand in the gap for America, where are the intercessors? The Holy Spirit is calling all true believers to cry out to God on behalf of our nation and then to cry out to our nation on behalf of God. Who will answer the divine call to stand in the gap for the United States? Who will answer the call to take up the lost ministry of intercession?

**four**

# THE ROCK THAT CANNOT BE SHAKEN

There is none holy like the LORD, there is
none besides thee; there is no rock like our
God.

—1 SAMUEL 2:2, RSV

## A Stable Place

The key to surviving an earthquake is to find a stable
place. Of course, the safest place to be when the ground
is shaking is in an airplane. In an earthquake, anything
that can be shaken is a danger to you. What is true in
the physical realm is also true in the spiritual realm. The
safest place to be during a "spiritual earthquake," is in
a place that cannot be shaken. God is calling the church
in the United States to be that place of stability where
Americans can find the safety of Christ Jesus.

Because of our turning away from the Lord, America
has experienced many tremors in recent years. As we
have drifted further and further away from God's heart,
His hand of protection has been progressively removed
from our country. If we continue our spiritual and moral
downward spiral, these tremors will only increase. God
has been faithful to send us powerful wake-up calls to
show us that we need Him. If we continue to reject His
mercy, His full wrath and judgment will surely fall.

The church in America has been given a divine

responsibility to share a message of stability with our country. In the last chapter we looked at one part of that responsibility, our intercessory prayer. If the church in America will now begin to stand in the gap on behalf of our land, the message of the Gospel will be clearly seen in America. Once we begin to experience God's burden for this country through intercession He will place His powerful anointing in our hearts and His wonderful message in our mouths. He will also allow the church to become that stable place our nation is looking for in the midst of the shaking.

## Christ, the Solid Rock

Even though we have experienced so much instability in America, there is wonderful news for our nation today: there is a place of stability where God wants us to find safety in the midst of the shaking. There is a place of complete peace, where God will protect us from the judgment taking place around us. This stable place is found only on the solid Rock of Christ Jesus. The old hymn rings true at this point, "On Christ the solid rock I stand, all other ground is sinking sand."[1] In this case, we might say that, "all other ground is shaking sand." God wants us to know that there is a stable place for us to stand during the shaking. The simple message of the Gospel has always been that, "There is no rock [of stability] like our God."

Even though our country has been violently shaken and unsettled, we can look to our Maker and find true peace and stability in Christ. God wants America to see there is hope for us still. Through all of the shaking that surrounds us, our hope is found in Jesus, the Rock that cannot be shaken. If the church in this nation will seek God as never before, He will use us to share this hope as never before. Jesus Christ is the only Rock that we can stand on and be safe from harm. The Bible makes this fact very clear. I don't really understand why more ministers, churches, and Christians in our nation do not take a stand on this issue. If the Word of God makes it clear there is only one way to the Father, then why can't the church make it clear to America? Perhaps we are too concerned with hurting people's feelings. We want everyone to feel that their views or opinions of God are all equally important. Jesus, however, has an entirely different message for us in the Bible. According to Him, there is only one way to get to our Creator God. He makes it crystal clear in the Book of John, "I am the way, and the truth, and the life; no one comes to the Father, but by me" (John 14:6, RSV).

## Safe in the Father's Arms

The Bible clearly shows the only way back into the Father's loving arms is through Jesus. Recently I took my family to Florida for a summer vacation. Two of my children in particular enjoyed our trip to the beach. It was the first time that either of them had seen the ocean. My son was very brave and he let me take him out into the water a little bit. Mom was not particularly thrilled about this venture, but we assured her that we knew what we were doing and we would be safe.

Out we went, until the water was a couple of feet deep. I held my son up over the waves and he marveled at the majesty of the vast ocean before us. In the hot Florida sun we both enjoyed the mist from the waves that sprayed the cool ocean water on us. Little did my son know that if I had not been taking care of him his life would have been in terrible danger. As a loving father, I held him firmly in my arms, above the dangerous pull of the ocean tide. If I would have let him go, the current from the waves would have immediately put his precious life in jeopardy. We returned from our adventure that day without any such misfortunes and God taught me a very important spiritual lesson.

America is not unlike my young son right now. We enjoy a splendid view of the "ocean" of the world while God's arms hold us just above the awesome pull of danger's tide. During our history we have been mostly sheltered from harm in the stable arms of an all-powerful God. Today in America, however, something is terribly wrong. It seems that we are now fighting with all that is within us to escape the grasp of our heavenly Father. With the lifestyles we live, the decisions we make, and the attitudes we have, we have fought against our Maker. Through our desire to get God out of our homes, our culture, and even our public places we are struggling against His loving grip. My friend, if these things continue it won't be long until the Lord will be forced to let us go.

Although everything in our world seems beautiful and peaceful at first glance, terrible dangers lie just beneath the surface. We have a loving, heavenly Father and His only desire is to take us in His arms and allow us to enjoy the glory of His creation. He wants to hold us up near His heart, above the dangerous pull of sin's tide just beneath us. God the Father has revealed this desire in the life of His only Son, Jesus. Through His sacrificial death on the cross, we can now come to the Creator of the universe as to a loving Father. Make no mistake about it, He longs for us to do this very thing. He is waiting with His strong but tender arms, to secure us and shield us from all in this world that would destroy. Listen to what the Bible has to say about this matter:

The eternal God is your refuge, and underneath are the everlasting arms.
—DEUTERONOMY 33:27, NKJV

## Spiritual Tremors

The church in America must return to the only Rock that cannot be shaken if we are going to reach this country with the love of God. Our theology is quite shaky in the American church. Many Christians have embraced a watered-down version of the Gospel. Somehow we feel we can be Christians and yet not offend anyone in the process; however, the Gospel by its very nature is offending—intelligently designed to comfort the afflicted and afflict the comfortable. For some reason we believe we can have a relationship with a loving and holy God and also have a relationship with the desires of this world. Through our lifestyles and our pulpits we have preached a perverted gospel to the United States. What we must see is that God will hold us accountable for living and teaching such a message.

I remember feeling the spiritual tremors recently at a funeral I attended. The person who had passed away was young and had lived a very sinful lifestyle. This was not simply a rumor or gossip, but all in attendance that day knew of this person's blatant ungodly lifestyle. The deceased had been living with a "partner" outside of marriage up until the time of his death. During the funeral service I watched in utter amazement as the minister began to share how this person was going to heaven. He stated that this individual had received a free ticket because of an altar call that took place years ago. Apparently, this person had come forward and shaken hands with the preacher at the front of the church. This individual had "accepted" Jesus as his personal Savior.

His lifestyle, however, demonstrated that Jesus was not the Lord of his heart at all.

I am certainly not the judge on such matters, but if it walks like a duck and it quacks like a duck, don't call it a chicken. We can never know the mercy and the love of God that has allowed millions of people to come to Him during the last hour of their lives. I believe there was time and an opportunity for this person to repent and accept the Lord. Whether or not he did this is not up to me to judge. We cannot base our declaration of people's entrance into heaven on a simple prayer that they prayed years ago if their life shows they did not really mean it. God is always the judge on such matters and let us be sure that He is full of mercy and compassion for the lost. The simple truth that the Father wants us to understand is that if Jesus is not both our Lord and our Savior, He cannot be either.

God wants all or nothing in our relationship with Him. He is not interested in a halfway commitment. Could it be that the minister who preached that young person's funeral that day will be accountable for the many people who "shook" hands with him, but were never told they needed to repent of their sin and truly live for Jesus? Listen to this passage from the Book of Ezekiel, "When I say to the wicked, 'You shall surely die,' and you give him no warning, nor speak to warn the wicked from his wicked way, to save his life, that same wicked man shall die in his iniquity; but his blood I will require at your hand" (Ezek. 3:18, NKJV).

I do not believe this preacher's salvation theology is an isolated case. The spiritual tremors from halfhearted commitments are raging through the church in America today. Could it be that the blood of thousands of sinners is on the hands of the American church? Through our lifestyles and our pulpits, we have told America they can live for God and live for themselves at the same time. The Bible, however, makes no such statements. We must return to the only message of stability in a nation that is unstable. Salvation is found only through a passionate faith relationship with Jesus Christ. He is the only One who can make the spiritual ground beneath us stable again. If Americans do not turn away from their sin and turn to Christ in faith, they can shake a thousand preachers hands and still split hell wide open.

## Being a Witness to America

If the church in America will climb back into our loving Heavenly Father's arms again, He will use us to call this nation back to Himself. We can once again return to the stable spiritual ground of the true Gospel. We can once again become a witness for Jesus in our land. In the Book of Acts, Jesus speaks of His desire to use us in this way:

> But you shall receive power when the Holy Spirit has come upon you; and you shall be witnesses to Me.
> —ACTS 1:8, NKJV

Another problem with many in the church in America today is that we are trying to be lawyers instead of witnesses. We are arguing with people and trying to convince them of the truth of the Gospel. We must remember that the only job a witness really has is to speak of what he has seen and heard. The lawyer's job is to argue the case and convince the jury. The witness's job is simply to bear testimony to what they have personally experienced. What America needs at this hour is not a church that is arguing the truth to them, but one that is simply "being a witness" for Jesus. Let us leave the "convincing of the jury" up to the Holy Spirit.

A witness can only testify to what they have personally seen and heard. The problem with many Christians in America is that we are no longer seeing and hearing. For many of us, it has been a long time since we have experienced anything spiritually significant. Yes, we talk about how God has saved us and we sing about what He has done for us, but how many of us are actually experiencing His presence on a daily basis? As a whole, we are a church in desperate need of revival. We need the fresh wind of the Spirit to blow through our lives once again and make us witnesses for Jesus. We need to become sensitive to the Lord once more so that He can work in our churches in a new way. I would venture to say that there are as many divisions in some of our churches as there are new converts and miracles. May we return to the stable spiritual ground of a daily experience with Christ.

## The Book of Acts Revival

The Book of Acts church was one that was planted firmly on the solid Rock of Christ. It was a church that was experiencing genuine revival. There were no halfhearted commitments in their ranks. They were powerful and relevant witnesses for Jesus in the wicked society in which they lived. I am not sure if they would get anything out of our hyped-up, cutting-edge, and technologically advanced meetings. They might ask us, "Where is the substance of God's presence?" They might wonder where the miracle-working power is, that shows the church as God's chosen dwelling place. Listen to me Christian, the church in the Book of Acts was a church in revival. Dare we think that Jesus is returning for a church less empowered and revived than the one He left?

Slick-haired preachers in $3,000 suits did not manufacture the Book of Acts revival, disgracing the Gospel by begging for money to fuel their multi-million dollar "ministry" machines. Those preachers who practice this today are insulting God's people by telling them, "Just plant a seed and God will meet your need." The Book of Acts contains no such "appeals." Many ministers need to stop making His house a house of money, and let it be a house of free miracles. These preachers need to stop insulting the grace of God and start freely offering the anointing that He has graciously placed on their lives. Perhaps they need to believe God to supply their ministry with enough money so that they won't have to manipulate His people with their crocodile tears.

The Book of Acts church did not use appeals or the latest marketing techniques to grow the work of the Lord. They were too busy trying to save their world from hell. They also understood that only God could grow His church. (See Matthew 16:18.) The Book of Acts revival was ushered in by the very presence of God, as His people sought Him in desperation. Do we realize how desperate they were? If the Holy Spirit did not show up and empower them to be witnesses for Christ, they were in big trouble: they were facing a ruling religious party that wanted every follower of Christ terminated.

## Revival's Proper Definition

With so much talk about and prayer for revival today in the American church, we must learn to recognize what it actually looks like. Otherwise we will be like the religious rulers in Israel two thousand years ago who were looking for their Messiah while persecuting the Lord's Messiah. We too can be guilty of looking for our revival while we ignore or even persecute the Lord's revival. There are three truths the Holy Spirit wants us to focus on as we look for genuine revival. Unless we see these three things, we cannot call what we experience genuine revival.

First, revival is Jesus returning to His rightful place in our lives as well as in our churches. (See Malachi 3:1–3.) Christ must have the preeminence in all things. Church really is supposed to be all about Jesus. Second, revival is believers returning to their first love. (See Revelation 2:4.) Many Christians are lukewarm or even spiritually cold in their love for God today in America. God is not interested in a halfway relationship, but in a faith that is pure and white-hot. Third, revival is the church returning to its normal state. (See Acts 4:31–33.) The Book of Acts church was one that preached the Gospel with power. The Spirit worked in a mighty way to bring assurance to all of the authenticity of the message the church preached.

Revival is God again restoring His church to spiritual purity and power. Some of us are not even looking for God to move in revival power because we have done one of two things to excuse our lack of revival. First, some of us have convinced ourselves that God simply doesn't move in power anymore. This line of thinking usually discounts modern-day miracles and any other powerful witnesses to the Resurrection of Christ. The thought is that these things are no longer necessary because we have the completed canon of Scripture now. I attended a Bible college that taught such foolishness. By convincing ourselves that God no longer moves in revival, we have grieved the Holy Spirit in our churches. Listen American Christian, if ever we needed the presence of the Holy Spirit, it is today. If ever we needed to show our nation solid proof that Jesus is alive, it is today. Are we so naive to believe that Jesus, "shewed himself alive after his passion by many infallible proofs" (Acts 1:3) to the early church, but that He is willing to do less today? May God help us if His power and glory are not the same today as they were two thousand years ago when He conquered death and hell for you and for me. He is the same awesome God, only we have changed. (See Hebrews 13:8.)

The second reason many are not seeking God for revival right now is that we have convinced ourselves we don't need it. We have our "pure" doctrine, we have our beautiful buildings, we have our dynamic expository sermons, and our catchy one-liners. We have the latest worship songs from around the world, sung by the most talented musicians and accompanied by awesome choirs and instrumentalists. Hey, this thinking makes sense: who needs the Spirit of God to visit our churches when we can be Christ's witnesses with our own talents? May God forgive us of our pride if we are not desperate for His glory to return to His church. We must remember it is the lukewarm (indifferent and complacent) church the Lord will spit out of His mouth. (See Revelation 3:16.)

## Those Who Are Desperate

God is looking for some Christians who are desperate for revival in America. When our hunger and desperation matches that of the Book of Acts believers, then we will see God move as they saw Him move. The early church was desperate for the presence of the Lord. As a result, they experienced a heaven-sent revival. The revival that I am talking about gave the Holy Spirit His proper place as the divine Leader of the church. This revival made Christ central to all that the church said and did. He was the solid Rock upon which their theology was built. Sin was called sin and it was preached against. The Holy Spirit made the presence of Christ so real that literally thousands of people were converted in meetings with no sound systems, mass choirs, or pre-trained altar workers. That is the kind of revival that is needed in America today. If it is available today, if God is willing to pour out His Spirit upon His children and visit us, if we can be witnesses for Christ in His power, then nothing else matters.

As I stated earlier, there are places where God is moving in America, but as a whole, revival is absent from the church in our nation. Millions of Americans are dying and going to hell while we try to decide if we want Christ to be the center of our churches or not. God has not left us without hope of a revival, however. In chapter 7, we will look at the revival that is coming to a desperate American church.

May the church in America listen to the shaking that is taking place in our country. May we intercede for our nation and proclaim God's message of hope and healing. May we allow Jesus to be the only Rock upon which we stand. May we call America back into the Father's arms through Christ. May we seek God for a revival that He is willing and able to send to the United States. May we be those who are desperate, in this hour, for God to pour out His Spirit upon the church in America.

# five

# A Glorious Church

That he might present it to himself a glorious church,
not having spot, or wrinkle, or any such thing; but
that it should be holy and without blemish.
—Ephesians 5:27

## God Is in Control

Through all of the shaking that has taken place in
America, the Lord is raising up His own special people.
Even though there are many who are lukewarm in the
church, some believers are now responding to the shaking. Although there are many houses of worship in the
United States that are being spiritually shaken, there is
also stability to be found. Many churches are returning to the Rock that cannot be shaken and to the firm
foundation of Christ. Above all else, we must remember
the church belongs to the Lord Jesus and He is a faithful
Shepherd during any time of distress. If we allow Him,
He will give us His perfect peace no matter the instability
which may surround us.

The church that Jesus will return for will be a glorious
church that is in full-blown revival. God is not raising up
a weak or feeble church, but a glorious church to meet
Jesus at His Second Coming. Even though our nation
and many churches in America are being shaken right
now, God is still working out His purpose. Scripture gives

us assurance that He is more than able to bring His good plans to pass in His church, even as His judgment falls upon the unrepentant:

> In whom also we have obtained an inheritance, being predestinated according to the purpose of him who worketh all things after the counsel of his own will.
>
> —EPHESIANS 1:11

What a comforting message for believers in America today. God is sovereign and in complete control at all times. Even when everything seems that it is spinning out of control and being violently shaken, we can rest assured that God is still on His throne. As Christians in America, this is the biblical message we must preach. If we are to change a nation that is trembling under the weight of divine judgment, we must see that God is still sovereign during the shaking. Let me again quote the words from an Old Testament prophet concerning this matter:

> I form the light and create darkness, I make peace and create calamity; I, the LORD, do all these things.
>
> —ISAIAH 45:7, NKJV

Things may seem as if they are out of control sometimes, but the Bible assures us that a loving and all-powerful God is always in complete control. He is able to work out His plan, even through those who have hardened their hearts against Him.

## Who Is to Blame?

God is good and loving and merciful, but He also judges sin with calamity. This is the paradox of God that is taught throughout the Bible and consistent with history. This does not mean we should blame God for the evil that comes upon us though. He never takes delight in judging sin, but rather delights in mercy. There is a great vacuum that is created when a society rejects the plan of God. When a person, people, or nation rebels against God, judgment is the only thing that can fill the empty void where the blessings of God should rest.

Another person whom we seek to place the blame of disaster upon is the devil. We American Christians tend to see satanic influence everywhere. Somehow we think he has more power than he actually does. All of the bad things that happen in the world are blamed upon the primary enemy of God. Do we really understand that Satan is destined for eternal damnation along with all who follow him? Do we know and believe that God, not Satan, created hell? Many still have a mental picture of the devil running around hell and sticking people with a pitchfork. The Bible gives us no such image, but assures of Satan's own judgment:

> And the devil that deceived them was cast into the lake of fire and brimstone, where the beast and the false prophet are, and shall be tormented day and night for ever and ever.
>
> —REVELATION 20:10

So we cannot simply blame the devil and his minions for all of the shaking in America today. In fact, God has more to do with it than Satan does. God is just and even though He longs for our fellowship through Christ, He will not allow rebellion to go unpunished in this life or the next. The devil is not gaining the upper hand in the cosmic struggle of good versus evil. He is not, as we believe, able to manipulate world events at his discretion. Yes, Satan is able to wreak havoc, but we must understand that God has him on a very short leash. God is good and brings judgment to the wicked in this life only so that people may turn to Him in faith and live their lives for Jesus Christ. In the midst of great calamity God is still in control and able to work out His plan through His glorious church.

American Christians must stop blaming the devil for the judgment that is taking place in our nation today. We must remember that God alone is the Lord of the nations. Even though the devil can influence people and events, we must see that his power is limited to that which God allows. God is teaching us that our choices have consequences. If America chooses to reject the reign of Christ, we will suffer the same judgment that fell on Satan when He rejected God's rule in heaven. (See Isaiah 14:12–15.) We must understand that it is not God who is troubling America, it is Americans through our rejection of His counsel.

## Focusing on God's Purpose

There is a wonderful purpose that God is bringing to pass in the American church right now. Even though our nation is being shaken with judgment, the Lord is working out His eternal plan through those who believe. What is God's purpose for the church in America? I can say with all assurance that many Christians in our country have missed what God wants to do through us in this hour of divine visitation. The church in America has been so busy being distracted by side issues that we can no longer hear God's heart speaking to us through the shaking. How do I know this? If you visit many churches in

America today, you will see spiritual pride at work.

While millions of Americans are headed for hell without Christ, we debate our doctrine. We emphasize our pet truths and focus on our distinctiveness, when all the while Christ's desire is for us to be unified around Him. While God's heart is breaking for the United States, ours is occupied with insignificant issues. We tear each other down over the use of certain words and doctrines that we view as sacred and we neglect the fact that Christ died to bring all of us into a place of oneness in Himself. (See John 17:20–21.) God has a purpose for all true believers in America during this hour. This purpose is not that we debate our distinctive beliefs and private interpretations of Scripture.

God's purpose is to change His church and then to change the society in which we live. So what does God want to change about the church? The issue is not one of doctrine or practice, the issue is a matter of the heart. God is not impressed with our doctrinal emphasis, our pet truths, or our individual and distinctive revelations of His Word. He is not impressed by our head-knowledge or our correct interpretation of Scripture. How we interpret the Bible is important, but there is something that is vastly more important in the eyes of our Savior. When He looks at His church, He sees something totally different than what we see.

## What God Is Looking At

> But the LORD said to Samuel, "Do not look at his appearance or at the height of his stature, because I have refused him. For the LORD does not see as man sees; for man looks at the outward appearance, but the LORD looks at the heart."
>
> —1 SAMUEL 16:7, NKJV

The Lord originally spoke these words of David, who was to rule in Saul's place as king over Israel. This verse does, however, contain a universal truth of how God sees people. When looking at His church in America today, God does not see what we see. God is impressed with the position of our hearts toward Him. If our hearts are not turned toward Him in faith and love, we can have all of our doctrine straight and still displease our Creator. The real issue is a matter of the heart. Although this book does contain much truth from the Word and there is a lot of biblical teaching in it, it is primarily a book from God's heart. The Lord had me write *The Shaking of a Nation* as a message from His heart to America, and specifically from His heart to the church in America.

The American church is altogether focused on the wrong things. How do I know this? I am a pastor. I can tell you from experience that the first question one pastor will ask another when they meet is, "How big is your church?" Ministers are so concerned with numbers and impressing each other with our influence, that we miss God's heart. Man looks at numbers; God looks at something much more valuable. Man looks at the beauty of the church building; God looks at the hearts of those inside. Man is impressed by large churches that do everything well; God is impressed with contrite hearts that cry out to Him. Man is impressed with doctrinal creeds and statements of faith; God is impressed with the passion of our faith in Christ. Man is impressed with the latest and greatest worship songs; God is impressed with the love and spiritual hunger in our hearts as we sing those songs to Him.

## A Church After God's Own Heart

Changing His people into a "Davidic church" is God's purpose for all true Christians in America. Please understand that I am not speaking of changing the names of our churches or even our denominational affiliation. The matters that I speak of are spiritual and they must be received as such. The "Davidic church" (named after King David of Old Testament Israel), is the Christ-centered church that brings to God the glory that is due Him. The "Saul church" (named after King Saul of Old Testament Israel) is the self-centered church that only seeks its own welfare and glory. The Lord wants us to see that there are two groups of Christians in America today (just as in any society). Although both groups wear the name "Christian," only one group is accepted in God's eyes.

Through all of the shaking in the United States, God is changing the character of His church. He is raising up the Davidic church and overthrowing the Saul church. Bear in mind that much of what was written in the Old Testament was written for our example and to teach us spiritual truths. (See 1 Corinthians 10:11.) A careful study of the lives of Saul and David in 1 and 2 Samuel will bring many of the things that I will discuss here into clear focus. I would encourage you to read some about Kings Saul and David right now, before you read the rest of this chapter.

For the purpose of what God is saying right now to the church in America, let us look to a New Testament Scripture concerning these two leaders of Israel. Consider the following passage from the Book of Acts regarding these two men:

> God gave unto them Saul the son of Cis, a man of
> the tribe of Benjamin, by the space of forty years.

> And when he had removed him, he raised up unto them David to be their king; to whom also he gave testimony, and said, I have found David the son of Jesse, a man after mine own heart, which shall fulfil all my will.
>
> —ACTS 13:21–22

## The Saul Church Versus the Davidic Church

From this passage it is very easy to see that God says He looked at the hearts of these two men. While one had His approval, the other did not. Let us apply this verse to the church in America today. According to Ephesians 2:6, the church is ruling and reigning with Jesus Christ in spiritual places. The Bible makes it very clear that we are "kings" in a spiritual sense. Just as in Old Testament Israel, the Saul church is after the flesh and it depends on itself. The Davidic church is after the Spirit and it depends on God. Christians, if you are able to receive it, this is what the Spirit is saying to the church in America today: He is removing the Saul church and raising up the Davidic church.

The Saul church has been concerned with its own glory and reputation. The Davidic church is concerned only with the glory and reputation of God. The Saul church is taller and better looking than the rest and it looks good on the outside. The Davidic church has the beauty of a heart after God and it doesn't seem too impressive to the world. The Saul church has all the best armor and military skill. The Davidic church fights its battles with only a sling and five stones (the Word, worship, prayer, faith, and love), and the Spirit of God guides these stones. The Saul church lives in the palace, loves the fine things in life, and loves being in the spotlight. The Davidic church sometimes lives in the caves of obscurity and seeming insignificance, but God's presence dwells with it there.

The Saul church has used its power to manipulate and control, so that it can attain its own purpose. The Davidic church knows its power comes from God and it is concerned with being controlled by the Spirit to achieve God's purposes. The Saul church is currently in power and sitting on the throne. All of the resources of the kingdom are available to it. The Davidic church is being overlooked, as it faithfully watches over the Lord's sheep in the field and it does the small things that God has given it to do. The Saul church hates and persecutes the Davidic church because of the anointing of God upon it. The Davidic church responds only with love and mercy, as David spared Saul's life when Saul sought to murder him. As Saul hurled his spear at David, so the Saul church attempts to kill the Davidic church with its words and accusations. The Davidic church responds only with forgiveness and would never stretch out its hand against the Saul church.

The Saul church is in the comfort of abundance and relaxed, as it sleeps in spiritual lethargy. The Davidic church is often overwhelmed and prays as David did, "How are they increased that trouble me! many are they that rise up against me" (Ps. 3:1). The Saul church places no value on the anointing and it is about to lose it, just as the Holy Spirit left Saul and he did not realize it. (See 1 Samuel 16:14.) The cry of the Davidic church is:

> Do not cast me away from Your presence, and do not take Your Holy Spirit from me.
>
> —PSALM 51:11, NKJV

## God Knows Who's Heart Is Really After Him

God is judging His church in America and it is time for the Davidic church to stand up and bless the Lord as King David did, with complete dependence upon God. The Lord will not stand for a church that depends upon itself to be His representative in a land that is being shaken. Jesus paid much too high a price with that precious blood that He shed for us at Calvary to have a church that is not sold-out to Him in America. Listen to this passage from the New Testament, calling believers to become who God intended us to be, leaving all iniquity to embrace Christ:

> Nevertheless the foundation of God standeth sure, having this seal, The Lord knoweth them that are his. And, Let every one that nameth the name of Christ depart from iniquity. But in a great house there are not only vessels of gold and of silver, but also of wood and of earth; and some to honour, and some to dishonour. If a man therefore purge himself from these, he shall be a vessel unto honour, sanctified, and meet for the master's use, and prepared unto every good work. Flee also youthful lusts: but follow righteousness, faith, charity, peace, with them that call on the Lord out of a pure heart. But foolish and unlearned questions avoid, knowing that they do gender strifes. And the servant of the Lord must not strive; but be gentle unto all men, apt to teach, patient.
>
> —2 TIMOTHY 2:19–24

Through all of the shaking and calamity that has been experienced in America, God has a message for the church. It is not the devil who has caused our instability, but God's judgment. It is not the Lord who is to blame for this judgment, but it is America, by our rejection of His will. God is raising up a people who are wholly dependant upon Him to be His witnesses to America. The Saul church cannot help the United States in her hour of need. Only the Davidic church, which understands God's heart, can bring comfort to a nation that is troubled. Only the Davidic church can be that place of stability where desperate Americans can take refuge in the Rock of Christ Jesus.

Remember that the Lord is in complete control over all of the events taking place in our country today. He wants His Davidic church to have peace in the midst of the storm that has engulfed America. There is a glorious purpose that God has for us, in speaking to the soul of a troubled nation. Let us be those who will rise up in America in her greatest hour of need and bring comfort and true peace. May we be willing for the Holy Spirit to change us into a glorious Davidic church. May we truly be a church after God's own heart.

## six

# HEALING OUR LAND

If my people who are called by my name
humble themselves, and pray and seek my
face, and turn from their wicked ways, then
I will hear from heaven, and will forgive
their sin and heal their land.
—2 CHRONICLES 7:14, RSV

## Judgment and Revival

In light of our sin and rebellion against God, what is His
plan for the United States? As the church experiences the
mighty revival that God is sending, America will have an
opportunity to return to her former glory. As I mentioned
earlier, this book contains a message of hope for all who
will hear. Yes, our nation has departed from our godly
heritage. Yes, we are guilty of many terrible national sins,
including the shedding of innocent blood. Yes, we have
experienced a divine wake-up call from the Lord through
the shaking in America. Through all of these things,
however, there is still hope for our country. This hope is
found only in Jesus and only in our turning back to God
through Him. It is not too late for America.

If the church will intercede and begin to stand in the
gap for the United States as God has called us to, a mighty
revival will result. The light of God always shines the
brightest during the darkest times of humanity. Through-

out history, when the evil of a society began to bring God's judgment, the Holy Spirit also began to bring revival. What we must understand is this revival in America must begin with the Christians. This revival will not start by itself, but it will start as a result of our response to the Lord. The only way that America can be spared, is if the true believers experience true revival. A heaven-sent revival will bring us back to our normal state of being a powerful witness for Christ in our nation. Just as in the Book of Acts church, the Spirit will again be given His proper place, prayer will be the order of the day, everything will be Christ-centered, and miracles will abound. Then our great nation will experience another great awakening and the Lord will heal our land.

## A Lesson in Revival From History

History tells us time and time again, that God always sends the most severe judgment right alongside with the most wonderful revival. Just when it seems there is no hope of restoration for a society, God visits His people once again. At the turn of the twentieth century, San Francisco was considered a very wicked place. A terrible judgment in the form of an earthquake occurred in April 1906 that destroyed much of the city. Thousands of people lost their lives, 225,000 residents became homeless, and 28,000 buildings were destroyed.[1] What has gone unnoticed by most historians is what happened during the same month on the other side of California.

Just when many Americans were hurting the most and wondering if there was any hope left, an awesome move of the Spirit began on the west coast. The "Azusa Street Revival" was one of the most powerful and far-reaching revivals of all time. Even after a century, its effects can still be felt today in the church worldwide. People came spiritually desperate and hungry from all across the globe in a time when travel took weeks and even months. Millions were touched as believers received a fresh experience with God and then took it back to their homelands. Many Christians entered into a new dimension of spiritual power as they received the baptism in the Holy Spirit. The Pentecostal movement that was birthed through this revival has been called, the "third force in Christendom" (the first being Pentecost and the second being the Protestant Reformation). It is now believed there are as many as five hundred million Christians who profess a Pentecostal/charismatic-type faith. From a powerful natural disaster alongside a spiritual awakening in California one hundred years ago, we can see that judgment and revival often come simultaneously.

## A Lesson in Revival From the Bible

Another powerful example we have of revival and judgment existing together can be seen in the Old Testament. The Book of 1 Kings sets the stage for some nation-changing events. After years of backsliding and compromise, Israel has completely forsaken the Lord. Baal is the chosen god that many of the Lord's covenant people are serving. King Ahab is reigning in the land and leading his people in idolatry. His wife Jezebel is considered to be one of the most evil women in history. Just when it seems Yahweh is going to totally reject His chosen race, along comes a prophet of the Lord. Elijah tells King Ahab it will not rain or even dew in Israel, except at his word. (See 1 Kings 17:1.) Thus a terrible judgment in the form of a famine begins in the land of Israel.

The ministry of Elijah was to bring the heart of his troubled nation back to the Source of every blessing. May I propose that God is now calling the American church to the same ministry? The United States is currently at the same place in its spiritual history as Old Testament Israel was in 1 Kings 18. The nation was completely given over to pride, greed, and lust and God was being rejected out of every aspect of society. The political and religious leaders did not recognize what was evil and what was good anymore. When it seemed hope was lost for Israel, God sent Elijah to proclaim an end to the drought. (See 1 Kings 18:1.)

The scene was dramatic. On Mount Carmel, the Lord Himself confirms the message that Elijah has been preaching by sending down fire from heaven. The false prophets of Baal cried out to their god for hours, with no result. Elijah simply prays a prayer in faith and God responds to him immediately and powerfully. Elijah then calls the people to completely destroy the false religion in Israel and a national revival begins. How we need the church in America to stand up today, like Elijah of old, and speak the Word of the Lord to the soul of a nation. If the church will now take up the mantle of Elijah, we will see the same results that Elijah did.

## An Abundance of Rain

After the Mount Carmel victory, Elijah made a significant statement. He said:

> There is a sound of abundance of rain.
> —1 KINGS 18:41

This was same prophet who had earlier pronounced the judgment of drought and famine upon the land. The amazing part of Elijah's faith was there was not a cloud in the sky, let alone the "sound of [an] abundance of rain." We must understand that Elijah was not just talking about physical rain, but also spiritual renewal.

Both of these types of rain refresh, both types renew, and both types come from heaven. Elijah was declaring the drought was over and God's blessing would now return upon a repentant nation. Now, again listen to the words of the Scripture that began this chapter, in its full context:

> When I shut up heaven and there is no rain, or command the locusts to devour the land, or send pestilence among My people, if My people who are called by My name will humble themselves, and pray and seek My face, and turn from their wicked ways, then I will hear from heaven, and will forgive their sin and heal their land.
> —2 CHRONICLES 7:13–14, NKJV

Let me give you the word of the Lord for America in this hour: there is now the sound of an abundance of rain over our land. Yes, it has been spiritually dry in many places for many years, but God has heard the prayers of the church for revival. Let us remember the same storm clouds that brought renewal to the land of Israel physically also brought revival spiritually. More importantly, these storm clouds brought judgment to the wicked government which immediately began to buckle under the weight of God's glory. God pronounced His intentions to remove the apostate government to Elijah in 1 Kings 19:15–18. His judgment upon Israel's government began to fall even as the rains of spiritual renewal and a great awakening descended.

The storm clouds now gathering over America are both for revival and for judgment. Revival is coming for the believer and judgment for the unrepentant. The finger of God is drawing a line in the dry spiritual dirt in our nation and it is time to decide where we stand. The storm clouds over America will bring awesome revival to the church and terrible judgment to the wicked (including our government) if there is no repentance.

## Preparing for Revival

Listen to these words from 2 Chronicles 7:14 one more time: "...if my people...shall humble themselves, and pray, and seek My face, and turn from their wicked ways." Let us notice the divinely-given steps to revival or "healing," for our land from this passage. Prayer is essential, but not just any prayer will bring revival and healing. Before the Lord mentions prayer he mentions humility. Humility is not something that we posses, but it is the position of our hearts toward our Maker. To put it simply, the word *humble* is a verb, not a noun. We are to humble ourselves and pray. We must understand that God does not hear all prayer, but only humble prayer. In fact, if we don't know Jesus Christ as our personal Lord and Savior, God won't even accept our prayer. This is the first part of humbling ourselves before God. We must come to the Father through the Son. Again, if you do not know the Lord in a personal way, you will be given detailed instructions on how to begin a relationship with Him in chapter 8. As we come humbly before the Lord in prayer, we are on our way to experiencing true revival.

Preparation for revival is both an instantaneous work of the Spirit and a lifelong pursuit. As we continually humble ourselves and come to the Father, we must develop the habit of prayer. Many of us know how to pray when we are in trouble. Yes, He may answer one on occasion to show us His love, but "emergency prayers" do not generally please God. No, we are called to something much more wonderful than this type of prayer. All true believers in Jesus are called to the habit of prayer.

The Creator of the universe is calling you and I to habitual communication and intimacy with Himself. What a wonderful blessing we can be to God, as we daily seek Him daily in earnest. Listen to the words of an authority on the subject of habitual prayer, the apostle Paul:

> Pray without ceasing. In every thing give thanks: for this is the will of God in Christ Jesus concerning you. Quench not the Spirit.
> —1 THESSALONIANS 5:17–19

We are told to make grateful prayer our constant habit. In fact, Paul says that if we do not do this, the Holy Spirit will be "quenched." The Holy Spirit can be rejected and His great love brushed aside. How? By neglecting to seek the Lord in prayer. The Spirit reveals to us there is a wonderful God who is longing and waiting for us to turn our hearts toward Him in habitual prayer.

The last preparation for revival mentioned in 2 Chronicles 7:14 is like a coin. Even though it is one thing in essence, it has two sides. The two sides of this coin are spiritual hunger and repentance. We are told to "seek" God's face and then we are told to turn form our "wicked ways." In our humble prayer we must have a hunger for the presence of the Lord and also a desire to be cleansed by Him. Many times we come to the Lord in prayer without spiritual hunger, asking only for what we need and want. Also, we often fail to seek God's face because we live in constant shame of who we are and what we have done. The simple truth is, if we will hunger after God and seek Him in faith, we would soon see our shortcomings fade into the background. This is the power of humble, hungry, and repentant prayer: it focuses our hearts on Jesus and takes our attention away from every bad and negative thing. When we humble ourselves through prayer and seek God in this way, we lay a firm foundation for revival. We invite the very presence of the Almighty to come and birth revival in our hearts.

## Feeding the Hungry by Fasting

The wonderful revival God is sending to our land will not fully materialize if believers will not pray in desperation. Many American Christians are falling short in the area of fasting. Fasting declares our hunger for God's presence. Through fasting we reach out to our Heavenly Father with our spirits and we tell Him that we desire His fellowship more than our natural food. We also open ourselves up to be a channel for the forgiveness and the love of God.

Fellow-Christians, America is hungry for God's mercy. Although we call ourselves the land of the free, we are actually bound by greed, lust, and pride. Though we enjoy wonderful physical freedoms, we are actually spiritual prisoners to our own desires. Millions of Americans are in bondage to greed and the love of money. We work longer and longer hours to acquire more and more "stuff" that can never fill a hungry soul. With great lust we covet our neighbor's car, property, and money. Our inward thought is that we would be happy if we just had this or that. Our pride has caused us to think and live like we will never stand before a holy God and give an account of what we have done with our time on earth. Our arrogance has caused us to think we are indestructible as a nation and now God is showing us that this in not the case.

Americans are hungry for the forgiveness and love of the Lord. There is only one way that they will be able to receive it—through the fasting of the church. Listen to what the Bible says about our ministry of fasting in Isaiah

58:6–7, "Is not this the fast that I have chosen? to loose the bands of wickedness, to undo the heavy burdens, and to let the oppressed go free, and that ye break every yoke? Is it not to deal thy bread to the hungry, and that thou bring the poor that are cast out to thy house? when thou seest the naked, that thou cover him; and that thou hide not thyself from thine own flesh?"

Many believers in our nation today have "hidden" themselves from their own flesh. Through our indifference, we have told our countrymen they can go to hell without Jesus. The Holy Spirit has a question for you, American Christian: *When was the last time that you humbled yourself and sought God's face through fasting for your nation?* What God wants us to see is that our sincere prayer and fasting will set the prisoners free and feed the hungry. If the church will cry out for America the Lord will undo the heavy burdens, and let the oppressed go free. If we begin to habitually fast and tell the Holy Spirit that we desire Him more than our necessary food, He will use our spiritual hunger to feed the soul of a nation. He will reveal His love and mercy to a country that is desperate for healing and forgiveness.

I pray to God that my fellow believers are not reading this book in vain. I pray you will surrender to the burden of the Lord that He is placing on your heart for America. I pray you will see that wonderful revival can be birthed through your desperation. I pray you will humble yourself and seek His face and turn from your apathy. Let you spiritual hunger feed thousands of Americans who are starving for the mercy of our loving Savior. Let your passionate prayers and faith be a part of the mighty revival that God sends to heal our land.

seven

# THE SHAKING OF REVIVAL

His voice then shook the earth; but now he
has promised, "Yet once more I will shake
not only the earth but also the heaven."
This phrase, "Yet once more," indicates
the removal of what is shaken, as of what
has been made, in order that what cannot
be shaken may remain. Therefore let us
be grateful for receiving a kingdom that
cannot be shaken, and thus let us offer to
God acceptable worship, with reverence and
awe; for our God is a consuming fire.

—HEBREWS 12:26–29, RSV

## God Is Moving Everywhere Else

During the hour of judgment that is upon our nation,
God is changing the hearts of all true believers. The Lord
is forming us into a Davidic church, that will follow hard
after Him. He is also placing the mantle of Elijah upon
us, so we can speak with authority to our beloved country. Through all of the shaking that God has brought to
our land, the church of Jesus Christ is receiving a kingdom that cannot be shaken. We are now being called to
offer acceptable worship to the Lord and stand in awe of
Him. At the same time God brings the healing of revival
to the American church, He will be working out a much
larger purpose that He has for us in this hour. The desire

of God's heart is that the church in America will become a prophetic voice that speaks to the nations.

*The greatest revival that the world has ever known is coming to America.* The Holy Spirit spoke these words to my heart recently. The day is coming when the glory of God will fall heavily upon America. Millions of people around the globe will be touched with the healing glow of revival fire that will burn brightly from our shores. This revival will bring everything back into proper perspective in American Christianity. Jesus will return to His rightful place as the center of our faith, doctrine, and worship. As Christ again takes the preeminence in all things, Christians will return to their first love. Finally, signs and wonders which glorify Jesus will abound as the church returns to its normal state of Spirit-empowered ministry.

Every believer who is thirsty for God in America soon will be satisfied. The hour is coming when the move of the Spirit in America will be so broad and so powerful, that halfway committed believers will be without excuse. There will be numerous places in every region, state, and city where this revival will burn brightly. All those who are truly hungry for the glory of God will have ample opportunity to seek Him where He is moving in power. Creative miracles will be commonplace in this revival, and millions will come to hear the message of the cross because of these signs that glorify Christ.

The Lord is tired of His people limiting what He can do in the United States. Many Christians today longingly talk about revival in far off lands. We talk about the huge open-air meetings and the mass conversions. We speak of the awesome miracles, which are confirming the Gospel and taking place on a regular basis. We say, "Well that is overseas, where God is free to move." I am here to tell you God is free to move wherever He wants, however He wants, and through whomever He wants. America's hour of divine visitation is at hand and it is time to believe that something wonderful from the Lord is finally upon us. If God were to show us the full magnitude of the work that He is about to do in America, we would have a hard time believing it. The day is coming when the revival in the United States will make Christians in other nations jealous for a similar revival.

## Wine, a Type of the Holy Spirit

When the day of Pentecost had come, they were all together in one place. And suddenly a sound came from heaven like the rush of a mighty wind, and it filled all the house where they were sitting. And there appeared to them tongues as of fire, distributed and resting on each one of them. And they were all filled with the Holy Spirit and began to speak in other tongues, as the Spirit gave them utterance. Now there were dwelling in Jerusalem Jews, devout men from every nation under heaven...And all were amazed and perplexed, saying to one another, "What does this mean?" But others mocking said, "They are filled with new wine." But Peter, standing with the eleven, lifted up his voice and addressed them, "Men of Judea and all who dwell in Jerusalem, let this be known to you, and give ear to my words. For these men are not drunk, as you suppose, since it is only the third hour of the day; but this is what was spoken by the prophet Joel: 'And in the last days it shall be, God declares, that I will pour out my Spirit upon all flesh, and your sons and your daughters shall prophesy, and your young men shall see visions, and your old men shall dream dreams; yea, and on my menservants and my maidservants in those days I will pour out my Spirit; and they shall prophesy."

—ACTS 2:1–5, 12–18, RSV

If we are to receive all that God is about to do in American Christianity, we must look to the Word of God and observe the pattern for revival. The authority for New Testament revival is the Book of Acts. Let us notice how the believers on the Day of Pentecost were mocked. While some were accepting the outpouring of the Spirit as being from the Lord, others were not. Some, to their own peril, were making fun of what God was doing in His people. Now here is a valid question: why did these mockers say that the believers were "filled with new wine?" (Acts 2:13, RSV). May I propose to you that these mockers were actually telling the truth? They were drunk with new wine, but not earthly wine. They were drunk with the reality of the presence of the Holy Spirit. How does a drunk person act? Of course speaking in tongues was a strange sign, but what other things were going on that day, as these first believers stumbled out of the upper room and into the streets of Jerusalem?

There is always an objection raised by mockers about spiritual manifestations. Certainly not all spiritual manifestations are of God, but are some? Of course. In fact, there is nothing that God does that Satan does not try to counterfeit. Excessive alcohol consumption is simply a cheap imitation for being drunk in the Spirit. What does one look like who is drunk on the reality of God's presence? There will be some of the same manifestations that we see in a person who is physically drunk: disorientation, staggering, laughing, crying, and perhaps a look on their face that says, "What is going on here?" We must not let these things offend us, but we must embrace them as being from the Lord. I hear the objections being raised by some revival watchers, "We need discernment." When religious people say things like this, it usually means that they would rather analyze what God is doing in others than to experience it for themselves.

The only discerning factor for whether or not something is of the Lord is this: if it brings glory to Jesus, it is God. If people are falling more in love with Jesus and His church, if the Word is becoming their passion once again and if they have a greater desire to be in God's presence, then rest assured the Holy Spirit is truly at work.

We must embrace what the Spirit is doing in America during this time of spiritual and physical shaking, or else we will suffer the same fate as the mockers on the Day of Pentecost. They were left out of what God was doing because of their unbelief. While the true church was experiencing the new move of the Spirit, these mockers stayed stuck in their religious tradition. Whenever believers begin to actually enjoy the presence of God, religious mockers always get upset. If people who are going to hell know how to party, how much more should we who are going to heaven? The coming revival will show our nation that God really does like to have a good time. He serves the best kind of wine last and throws the best parties for His children. We must not become offended by the new move of God as some of the Jews who were visiting Jerusalem did, during the Day of Pentecost.

## The Best Wine for Last

The power and love of God that is about to be released in the church in America, and then around the world, will make all other revivals pale in comparison. The first miracle that Jesus ever performed was prophetic in nature. I have often been puzzled at why our wonderful Lord would choose to turn water into wine for His first miracle. There were no doubt many sick people whom He could have healed. There were probably some who were at this very wedding in desperate need of a touch from God. Instead, the Lord chose to turn water into wine. This was a miracle many of us church people would consider to be very secular at best and perhaps even sinful, if it weren't for the fact that the sinless One performed it. Listen to the result of this miracle and what the master of the feast said to the bridegroom after Jesus turned the water into wine:

> And he said to him, "Every man at the beginning sets out the good wine, and when the guests have well drunk, then the inferior. You have kept the good wine until now!"
>
> —JOHN 2:10, NKJV

There is a prophetic message in this verse from the second chapter of John. I am here to tell you the Bridegroom is coming back soon. Jesus is coming back to catch away His church and He is not coming back for a people less revived than the church which He left. For almost two thousand years we have lived in a Last Days outpouring, and the Book of Acts has never ended. However, right before Jesus returns the revival in America and the rest of the world is going to be so much more powerful than anything the Book of Acts ever recorded. Mass healings will take place, where thousands of creative miracles will occur at once, with nobody laying hands on anyone. Of course the practice of laying hands on the sick is biblical, but the Lord is about to lay His own hands upon His church and upon our meetings.

This awesome outpouring and the accompanying signs will be a powerful witness to the reality of the presence of Jesus (see Acts 1:8), which is the point of all heaven-sent miracles. The greatest miracle of this revival will be the unity the Holy Spirit will bring. Christians from every church and denomination will shed their identity with that body to be identified with the body of Christ as a whole. There will be no containing the crowds that will come, not to a creed, not to a denomination, not to a doctrine, but to Jesus Himself. As Jesus is lifted high above all else, the anointing will flow as never before in His body. Any believer who chooses a creed or denomination over the presence of God will suffer loss and not gain. God has saved very His best wine for last. He is by no means going to pass by the church in America with this one last outpouring, but we will be instrumental in bringing this new wine to the nations.

## A Name and a Place for This Revival

Man always wants to put a label on what God is doing. We must realize that when we label an outpouring of the Spirit, we then limit the God who sends revival. Since God is without limit and His power is beyond our comprehension, we would do well to yield to what He is doing instead of labeling what He is doing. Many revivals in America have been labeled during their existence. Such was the case with the Great Awakening, the Azusa Street Revival, the Healing Revival, the Charismatic Renewal, and more recently the Brownsville Revival. Most revivals have been named by man and have therefore been limited to a specific time or location. Although every heaven-sent revival starts out as a work of the Spirit, eventually it gets labeled and becomes limited to a certain movement or group. When this happens, God seeks a new wineskin into which He can pour His new wine.

The Lord will remedy this labeling problem in the coming awakening. There will not be one church in particular to which everyone will be able to point to and say, "That is where this revival began." It will begin suddenly and spontaneously in many places of Christ-centered worship. In fact, Christ-centeredness will be the only prerequisite for this revival. It will transcend geographical, cultural, denominational, and ethical lines in America. Just as there will not be one particular physical epicenter for this revival, there will not be one preacher in particular who will be known as the leader of this revival. There will be many ministers who will flow in this new move of God, but the only "Superstar" of this revival will be Christ Himself.

## Persecution Restored

It is a fact that where God is moving the most, persecution is also the most intense. Just as in the Book of Acts, this world's systems (social, political, and religious) are trying to put out the fire that God has lit. This of course cannot be done. In fact, whenever persecution comes against the church, the fires of revival burn even brighter. What God does cannot be sidetracked or deterred by the rage of man. I am not sure what form of persecution will be coming to the church, but I know in my heart that it is coming very soon. However, we need not fear anything that man, inspired by the devil, may plot against God's people. We as Christians have that Someone much more powerful living in our hearts and He will take care of us through any test.

One of the places where persecution has been intense is the Far East. I will not mention the specific name of this nation here, but there is an Asian country where God's people are not given any freedom to worship in any form. All churches must be registered with, and thus controlled by, the government of this country. The amazing blessing is that the fire of revival is burning brightly in this same nation. We must understand that when the hand of the Lord comes upon a people to empower them as His church, persecution naturally comes as well. I don't know what kind of attacks will be leveled against the church in America, but I do know that they will be in direct proportion to the move of God that we experience.

Let us have faith that God is able to send revival to the United States of America. Let us not be as those who would analyze or mock this new move of God, but let us test it by the Spirit and enter in ourselves. Let us not seek to name or label this revival and thus limit God. Let us also be prepared for the persecution that will inevitably come as the Lord revives His people. The revival that is coming upon our nation will not only change our homes, our churches, our communities, and our government, but it will impact the nations. The fire of this revival will spread literally around the world until the entire earth has been touched by the glory of God as He impacts our nation with the shaking of revival.

## eight

# A BLESSED FUTURE

> Blessed is the nation whose God is the LORD;
> and the people whom he hath chosen for his
> own inheritance.
>
> —PSALM 33:12

## Biblical Blessing

We must understand that America has not been completely blessed by the Lord because we have not completely obeyed His voice. Yes, we have had an abundance of material wealth, but this does not mean God is blessing America. The "blessing" found in Psalm 33:12 implies complete divine favor in all areas of a nation's existence. When a nation is in this state of favor, God's blessing can be seen materially, but more importantly it can be seen spiritually, emotionally, and physically as well. This total divine national blessing can be found in the Book of Deuteronomy. Read the following passage with an open heart and understand that this is God's deepest desire for America:

> And it shall come to pass, if thou shalt hearken diligently unto the voice of the LORD thy God, to observe and to do all his commandments which I command thee this day, that the LORD thy God will set thee on high above all nations of the earth: and all these blessings shall come on thee, and overtake thee, if thou

72

shalt hearken unto the voice of the LORD thy God. Blessed shalt thou be in the city, and blessed shalt thou be in the field. Blessed shall be the fruit of thy body, and the fruit of thy ground, and the fruit of thy cattle, the increase of thy kine, and the flocks of thy sheep. Blessed shall be thy basket and thy store. Blessed shalt thou be when thou comest in, and blessed shalt thou be when thou goest out. The LORD shall cause thine enemies that rise up against thee to be smitten before thy face: they shall come out against thee one way, and flee before thee seven ways. The LORD shall command the blessing upon thee in thy storehouses, and in all that thou settest thine hand unto; and he shall bless thee in the land which the LORD thy God giveth thee. The LORD shall establish thee an holy people unto himself, as he hath sworn unto thee, if thou shalt keep the commandments of the LORD thy God, and walk in his ways. And all people of the earth shall see that thou art called by the name of the LORD; and they shall be afraid of thee. And the LORD shall make thee plenteous in goods, in the fruit of thy body, and in the fruit of thy cattle, and in the fruit of thy ground, in the land which the LORD sware unto thy fathers to give thee. The LORD shall open unto thee his good treasure, the heaven to give the rain unto thy land in his season, and to bless all the work of thine hand: and thou shalt lend unto many nations, and thou shalt not borrow. And the LORD shall make thee the head, and not the tail; and thou shalt be above only, and thou shalt not be beneath; if that thou hearken unto the commandments of the LORD thy God, which I command thee this day, to observe and to do them: and thou shalt not go aside from any of the words which I command thee this day, to the right hand, or to the left, to go after other gods to serve them.

—DEUTERONOMY 28:1–14

Notice the condition for receiving this type of blessing is obedience to the Lord. This divine favor will not fall upon any individual, group, or nation by chance. It will come only as we respond to the voice of the Lord by faith. It is the blessing that only comes to the heart that is turned completely to the Lord in faith and love. To receive this blessing, America is not expected to keep the Old Testament Law as Israel was required. We are, however, expected to hear and obey the voice of the Lord. What is God saying to America? It is time to return to our roots as a nation that honors God and obeys the Gospel of Jesus Christ. It is time to end the shedding of innocent blood. It is time for the church in America to fast and pray until the hearts of our leaders are changed and we bring our government back into line with the Word of God.

## From America to the Nations

When America's heart turns back to the Lord in faith, He will use us in an awesome way. Instead of American Christianity being known as stagnate and ineffective, it will be known as an awesome spiritual force which God uses to bring healing to the nations. We must obey the voice of the Lord in America. The church must be the first to respond by becoming a Spirit-empowered, Christ-centered people once again. The Bible tells us that:

> With great power the apostles gave witness to the resurrection of the Lord Jesus.
>
> —ACTS 4:33, NKJV

I believe the Lord wants it to be said of the church in America, "With great power the believers in America gave witness to the resurrection of the Lord Jesus." How we need the Holy Spirit to empower the American church to burn brightly for Jesus. Only then can America come back to the state of total divine blessing, which God created us to experience.

In popular culture it is safe to say that, "as goes America, so goes the world." Even though many hate our freedom, much of the world admires America. Many nations and cultures literally imitate our trends and styles. My question is, "What could God do with that influence if the church of the Lord Jesus became infused with the life-changing power of the Holy Spirit once again?" What an awesome thing that God could do with a country of passionate Christians who were no longer willing to embrace a perverted gospel, but who embraced the love and power of God again. We need revival in America today. Rest assured that God understands this. The question is not, "Will God revive the American church?"; the question is, "Will we individually choose to be a part of revival in America?"

## A Message for Those in Need of Christ

If you do not currently have a personal relationship with God, you can begin one now. Rest assured this book has found its way into your hands by divine providence. The Lord is calling to you through all of the shaking that has taken place in America in recent years. Have you heard His voice? He is telling you that He wants you to find peace and stability in Him. He is your Rock that cannot be shaken in an unstable world. He is calling you to enter into a passionate relationship with Jesus Christ. Through this book, He is not only calling you to be His child, but to share His heart for America. If you ask Him in faith, He will place His burden in you and give you the heart of an intercessor. As you follow the great Intercessor, Jesus, you will see awesome results take place through your prayers because you have chosen to stand in the gap before Him on behalf of the United States. His desire is for you to be a part of the great revival He is sending to America.

The question I have for you is, "Do you know Him?" Many people go to church faithfully, but they are not involved in a faith-relationship with the Lord. The question is not, "Do you know about God?" Many people can quote the Bible and tell you who God is, but salvation is more than that. Salvation is knowing the Lord in a personal and real way. It is believing in Him with all of your heart. It is taking His Word, the Bible, at face value and believing that every page contains God's inspired message for all mankind. Salvation is complete and total belief and trust in the Lord. Without this trust, it is impossible to surrender to the lordship of Christ. Without surrender to the lordship of Christ, it is impossible to be saved.

## Today Is the Day of Your Salvation

The good news is that you can begin or renew your personal relationship with the Lord right now. The Bible makes it clear that today is the day of salvation and now is the time to respond to the Lord. (See Hebrews 3:7–11.) Do not wait until the shaking in America and in your life gets worse before you respond to Jesus, but let today be your day of salvation. Listen to what the apostle Paul has to say on the subject of salvation from the Book of Romans. Let the simplicity of this verse sink deep into your troubled heart:

> But what does it say? "The word is near you, in your mouth and in your heart" (that is, the word of faith which we preach): that if you confess with your mouth the Lord Jesus and believe in your heart that God has raised Him from the dead, you will be saved. For with the heart one believes unto righ-

teousness, and with the mouth confession is made unto salvation. For the Scripture says, "Whoever believes on Him will not be put to shame.'"
—Romans 10:8–11, nkjv

Very simply put, you can be saved right now, from the payment and penalty for your sin. By coming to Christ and confessing that He is the Lord of your life, you can freely receive the benefits of the salvation that He accomplished for you at Calvary. There was a sin-debt that we all owed and that none of us could pay, but at the cross Jesus paid it all for us. By confessing He is Lord and putting your complete trust in Him and His work, you can receive the eternal benefits of the salvation that He purchased for humanity two thousand years ago. Today can be your day of salvation and right standing with God.

## Come Just As You Are

All true believers in Christ understand that we can do nothing to save ourselves or to "clean up our act" before coming to God. We are all guilty in God's eyes, because we have all chosen our will above God's will at some point in our lives. The wonderful message of the cross is that we do not have to "do" anything to earn our right standing with God. We can be made righteous simply by placing our faith in who Christ is and in what He did for us at Calvary. He was our substitute and now He is the One who is calling us home to the Father of mercy to find peace with God. The Scripture clearly teaches we need not try to improve ourselves to find God, but He accepts us just as we are. Listen to this verse from Revelation:

> The Spirit and the Bride say, "Come." And let him who hears say, "Come." And let him who is thirsty

come, let him who desires take the water of life
without price.
—REVELATION 22:17, RSV

The simple message God wants us to hear is "come."
You can bring all of your emotional and spiritual burdens to Christ today. You can come with all of your sin,
with all of your shame, with all of your guilt, with all of
your doubt, with all of your fear, with all of your depres-
sion, with all of your pride, with all of your hurt, with all
of your pain, and with all of your disappointments. The
Father is waiting for you and He longs for you to come
close to His heart through what His Son accomplished
for you on the cross. Whatever your burden is, you can
lay it at the feet of Jesus today and find true rest. He is
speaking to your heart right now of His desire to give you
peace. Listen to the words of the Savior:

Come to Me, all you who labor and are heavy laden,
and I will give you rest.
—MATTHEW 11:28, NKJV

Don't let anyone rob you of the simplicity of becoming
a Christian. There are many churches that teach you must
earn God's forgiveness and favor, but this is not what the
Bible teaches. God will receive you and forgive you just as
you are and right where you are. You can come to Christ
right now because of what He did for you on the cross of
Calvary. He longs for you to become one of His children.
When you respond to His call of salvation, you will be able
to hear and discern His voice. The more time you spend in
His presence and in His Word, the more you will learn to
know when He is speaking to you. He longs to show you
His plans for your life and how your faith in Him can influence the course of your family, your community, and your

nation. Jesus is calling you now—will you simply come to Him today?

## America Must Listen to the Shaking

Although our nation has been shaken there is still hope for America. God is speaking to us during the hour of our calamity. He is doing this because He wants us to avoid the coming judgment and experience His favor instead. He wants the United States to be known as a Christian nation again. Although terrible events have shaken us as a country, something much worse is on the horizon if we do not repent for our turning away from the Lord.

Now is the hour for all true believers in Jesus to rise up and repent for the sins of the United States. Now is the time for us to let our prayers be heard in heaven and our voices in the streets of our country, so judgment can be averted. How many Americans must truly repent and humbly turn to the Lord in order that our nation may be spared judgment and given mercy? Only heaven knows that answer, but rest assured the Lord is looking upon the heart of every American. He is calling each one of us to come to Him through faith in Jesus Christ and begin interceding for a nation that is on the brink of even greater judgment than we have known.

There can be no compromise on the issue of *Roe v. Wade*. It absolutely must be overturned if our nation is to be spared the full weight of God's justice. God's desire is not new legislation that limits certain types of abortion or new parental consent laws. He is calling the United States to have a complete change of heart and mind toward Himself. Every American must make their prayers to be heard in heaven and their voices heard throughout our government.

Every God-fearing American, our president, his advisors, every congressman and senator, every judge, and every leader in every branch of our government must now cry mightily unto God on behalf of our land. We must demonstrate our faith in Him by completely ending the shedding of innocent blood. As the king of Nineveh said thousands of years ago, so every American must now say:

> Who can tell if God will turn and repent, and turn away from his fierce anger, that we perish not?
> —JONAH 3:9

We must remember that whenever God speaks to us of His judgment, it is because He wants us to experience His mercy. God's desire is not destruction, but restoration. The Lord will heal our nation and bring us back to our rightful place of blessing if we will respond to His call and put Him first in all things. He longs to use every Christian and every church in the great revival that is coming upon our land. He longs to use America to spread revival to the nations of the earth. Listen to the words of Jeremiah the prophet, which apply to America today:

> "For I know the plans that I have for you," declares the LORD, "plans for welfare and not for calamity to give you a future and a hope."
> —JEREMIAH 29:11, NAS

It is time for America to listen to the shaking. It is time for us to hear the voice of the Lord as He speaks to us through the calamity that has come upon us. We have strayed so very far from our godly heritage. We have used our freedom to push God out of every aspect of American life. We have taken our God-given liberty and used it to murder millions of our own innocent children. If we do not end the shedding of innocent blood, worse judgments will fall soon. The call of the hour is for the true church to stand in the gap for America. We must cry mightily unto God on behalf of our beloved country. We must end the foolishness that has crept into our churches and become the united body of Christ once again. It is time to allow Christ to be the center of all that we say and do. If we heed the voice of the Lord in this hour, God will use us as part of another great awakening in the earth. God wants every Christian in America to embrace the new move of His Spirit, as He sends a mighty revival. If we will each do our part and repent of our national sin and turn to the Lord, we can once again be known as a glorious Christian nation.

Who will answer the divine call of the hour in America? Who will allow their heart to be broken with the things that break the heart of God? Who will stand up and fight for the cause of the innocent? Who will sound the alarm for America to hear? Who will become the prophetic church of Christ, and proclaim sure judgment and revival? Who will be a part of the coming awakening in the United States? Who will listen to what an all-powerful, yet loving and merciful, God is saying through the shaking of a nation?

> If that nation against whom I have spoken turns from its evil, I will relent of the disaster that I thought to bring upon it. And the instant I speak concerning a nation and concerning a kingdom, to build and to plant it, if it does evil in My sight so that it does not obey My voice, then I will relent concerning the good with which I said I would benefit it. "Now therefore, speak to the men of Judah and to the inhabitants of Jerusalem, saying, 'Thus says the LORD: "Behold, I am fashioning a disaster and devising a plan against you. Return now every one from his evil way, and make your ways and your doings good."'"
>
> —JEREMIAH 18:8–11, NKJV

# NOTES

**two**

## A Divine Warning
1. Abortion statistics and map from National Right to Life research, public domain. For more information see www.nrlc.org.

**four**

## The Rock That Cannot Be Shaken
1. Words from the hymn "The Solid Rock," by William Bradbury and Edward Mote, public domain.

**six**

## Healing Our Land
1. Statistics for the San Francisco earthquake taken from U.S. Geological Survey, Earthquake Hazards Program Web site, accessed 2/16/06: http://quake .wr.usgs.gov/info/1906/casualities.html.

To contact the author:


Pastor David P. Hill Jr.
P. O. Box 205
San Saba, TX 76877

www.shakingofanation.org